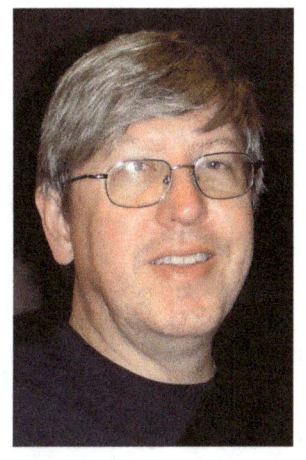

James A. Terry was born in Selma, Alabama in 1960. The son of a United Methodist pastor, he lived in several towns in central and south Alabama before graduating from high school in Mobile in 1979. James attended college and graduated with a history degree and a mathematics degree from Birmingham-Southern College. He went on to earn a Masters and PhD in Biomedical Engineering from the University of North Carolina – Chapel Hill. He worked as an Associate Professor at Tulane University for fifteen years teaching physics to radiology residents. James started a medical physics consulting firm, Enterprise Physics, LLC, and ran it for another fifteen years before selling it and moving to Pensacola, Florida. Currently he writes novels and recently became a Certified Prescribe Burn Manager – coursework completed at the Alabama Fire College in Tuscaloosa this past July.

Donald Olivares is a lifelong New Orleanian. He is the youngest of 5 siblings, born to parents who emigrated from Honduras in the late 1950s. His love of photography began on a family road trip from New Orleans to San Pedro

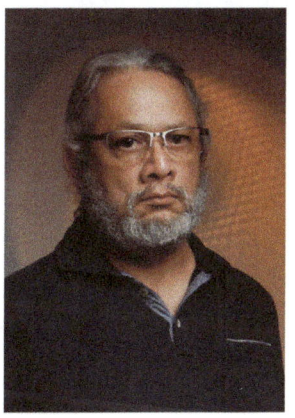

Sula, Honduras in 1973 where he took numerous photos with the family camera. He has been an employee of Tulane University for over 30 years in a variety of positions, his most recent is Clerkship Coordinator for medical students of the Radiology Department. Donald has been married to his wife, Amy for over 36 years. They have one son, Leo.

James Thomas Terry was born in Hale County, Alabama in 1934 and was raised at a place that came to be known as Peach Tree Farm. He joined the Moundville Methodist Church in 1945 and later graduated from Hale County High School. Tom farmed with his father, Willam F Terry, Sr., for two years after graduation, but soon felt the call to ministry. To prepare for this, he attended Birmingham-Southern College to get a Bachelor's Degree and then he went on to earn his Masters of Divinity from Vanderbilt University, serving churches as a pastor while at both institutions. Tom, as he was known to everyone, was a preacher in the United Methodist Church for more than fifty years. He was appointed to seven congregations in Hale County, including the Moundville and Stewart United Methodist churches in the 1990s. In 2001, he retired to the Moundville farm where he was raised (though he was pulled back into the ministry shortly thereafter, retiring again in 2003 and finally in 2007). Tom went on to farm cows there with George Tucker and George's dog, Katy. In these farming years, he planted the only peach orchard in Hale County, and for over a decade, he grew and sold twenty varieties of peaches.

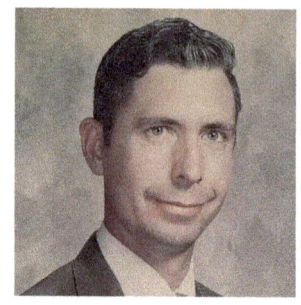

The sermons that Reverend Terry wrote over his five-decade career, were delivered in Tennessee and Alabama at more than two dozen small and large churches. Twelve of his sermons are now recorded in this new book, *Good News from Hale*, which also includes over thirty photographs of Hale County by New Orleans photographer, Donald Olivares. The book will be available in two bound versions as well as an e-book version.

GOOD NEWS FROM HALE

SERMONS OF J. THOMAS TERRY
AND
PHOTOGRAPHS BY DONALD OLIVARES

Edited by

JAMES TERRY

EnerPower Press
Cantonment, Florida
2025

Cover Image: Donald Olivares, Jr.

Paperback ISBN: 978-1-63199-952-9
Hardcover ISBN: 978-1-63199-953-6
eISBN: 978-1-63199-954-3

EnerPower Press
1241 Conference Rd
Cantonment, FL 32533

enerpowerpress.com
pubs@energion.com

CONTENTS

PREFACE TO THE TEXT

These are a remnant of the sermons given by my father over some fifty years as a United Methodist minister in Alabama and Tennessee.* I say remnant because only these twelve were found of what were surely hundreds given. Still, I think these are more or less typical. The specific dates and churches where they were delivered is unknown to me.

If you find that the text defies standard rules of writing, you can be sure that it was my choice to leave it as I found it - as lightly edited as possible. These sermons were meant to be spoken, not written. Any awkwardness can be removed by reading them aloud.

My father once told me about a young minister who asked a seasoned bishop what should he preach about. The bishop paused and said, "Preach about God. Preach about twenty minutes." I think you will find these twelve works conform to those rules.

The final sermon is most unusual in that it was delivered, so far as I know, (since I didn't hear this one personally) with no biblical references to support the message. I would argue that this sermon needs no reference since its meaning comes around to the very essence of Christ's teachings. (But I am obsessively drawn to consistency and felt compelled to find a biblical text, so I chose one and added one at the end.) For context, it must have been delivered in or around January of 1983, well after the Vietnam War ended but before the end of the Cold War.

---

*   He joined the Moundville Methodist Church in 1945 and was admitted into the Alabama West Florida Conference in 1955. He was ordained Deacon in 1958 and Elder in 1960. In 1966 he was selected the Rural Minister of the Year.

PREFACE TO THE PHOTOGRAPHS

    The photographs included in this volume were taken over six months in 2024 and 2025 in Hale County Alabama. Made more than five years after his death, they are independent impressions of Hale County and not inspired by the sermons per se. Hale was where James Thomas Terry was born, raised, frequently visited, and ultimately retired; these images are a reflection of the county and the land that Tom loved.

Editor's and Photographer's Dedication

To our fathers: Tom and Carlos

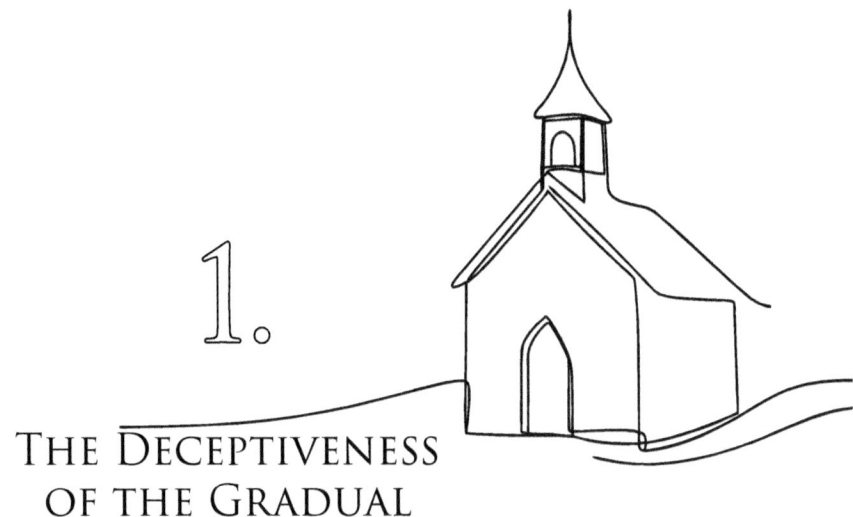

1.

THE DECEPTIVENESS
OF THE GRADUAL

Proverbs: 6:6-11
Go to the ant, you sluggard; consider its ways and be wise! It has no commander, no overseer or ruler, yet it stores its provisions in summer and gathers its food at harvest. How long will you lie there, you sluggard? When will you get up from your sleep? A little sleep, a little slumber, a little folding of the hands to rest - and poverty will come on you like a thief and scarcity like an armed man. (NIV)

Acts: 27:27-29
On the fourteenth night we were still being driven across the Adriatic Sea, when about midnight the sailors sensed they were approaching land. They took soundings and found that the water was a hundred and twenty feet deep. A short time later they took soundings again and found it was ninety feet deep. Fearing that we would be dashed against the rocks, they dropped four anchors from the stern and prayed for daylight. (NIV)

When I was a student in high school I lived on a farm and I took agriculture and I endeavored to learn as much as I could about the process of growing things from the soil. And one of the things that I learned when I was in school was that the six or eight inches that we have called topsoil is the most precious commodity that we have. Because, without it there would be no life on this earth as we know it, and it is easy for us to lose that precious commodity of topsoil if we do not watch. It can be eroded away. And there are basically two forms of erosion that removed the topsoil from where it is and we lose its effectiveness.

One is called gully erosion. When there comes a real big rain and there comes more water flowing and falling than the terraces and the contours can handle then something happens and the water spills over the contours or the terraces and it washes the topsoil away in a spot down to the subsoil. And I can recall as lad going out with my father on many occasions after the rain to see if the terraces had held or if one had broken and we had lost the topsoil.

The other way is called sheet erosion. It is when a drop of rain picks up a particle of soil and moves it a fraction of an inch down the hill. At first you think that is not much erosion. But I came to find out there is a greater loss of topsoil in our Southland through sheet erosion than there is in any other form of erosion. A tiny drop of water picking up a tiny grain of sand and moving it a fraction of an inch down the hill. It is so deceptive because it is so gradual.

And as I think about this, I begin to think about how it is in life that it is the deceptiveness of the gradual that causes us to be moved away from the things that are important and are meaningful and that are rich and that are renewing in our lives. It is so easy for us to be deceived by the gradual.

For a few moments I would like for us to think together about the things in our lives. The things in our Christian life that we have to guard against. The erosion of the principles and the things of life that give meaning and purpose to life to keep them from being eroded by the gradual.

First of all, there is the gradual feeling that we don't need God. I suppose that if there is anything that has affected the moral condition of our country, the spiritual condition of our country, in the last hundred years it has been the awareness of our power and our strength and might and our wealth. There comes the gradual feeling that we don't need God like we used to need God.

It is so easy to look around and say, "With all our wealth and with all of our comfort and with all of our food, with all of our security, what can God give us?" It is so easy for us to gradually drift away from our awareness of our need for God in our lives.

We have come to the realization that our minds can grasp what those before us could not grasp. Our hands can make with those before us could not make. We can use all of God's creation and it is so easy to forget that we still need him. And yet, I would remind us that we as God's children need him more today more than we ever have.

This generation stands in greater need of God's presence in our lives than any generation that has ever lived before us. First of all, because in our generation we have learned how to destroy the world unless we learn to live together. We have learned how to bring an end to life as we know it unless we learn to live together as brothers and sisters in Christ Jesus. And we can't learn to live together simply by ourselves, but we need the God who loves and cares for us to guide us. So, that is one reason that we need God more than any other generation has ever needed God.

Secondly, we begin to face the awareness that we may run out of some of the natural resources that we have become comfortable with and call our own and think that they will never end. We are beginning to face, in the field of energy, the fact that we are going to have to find some new sources or we are going to have to stop living quite the way we are living now. We have not yet come to grips with this. We have toyed with the idea for a few years, but it is something that is going to become a reality unless we deal honestly with it.

Or, look at the problem of ecology, we have learned how to make so many things scientifically that we have polluted the air and we have polluted the water and we have polluted the land. And unless we learn how to reverse this cycle, the day will come when this planet is not fit for human habitation. And so, we need God's guidance.

In human relations I've already mentioned that unless we learn to live together as brothers and sisters we shall not live at all. I stop and I look at our problems that we have in our world. I think of the emotional stress and strain in our world. The emotional stress in today's time is greater than any other period in history as far as I can fathom. Half of the hospital beds of America today are used for emotional recuperating because of the pressures of the world that are on us. And surely we must face the fact that we need God in the deep and abiding sense that we have never faced that we need before.

And yet, the deceptiveness of the gradual is that we have enough. Enough of things, enough of power that we don't need him. How deceptive it is.

The second dimension of the gradual is not only are we deceived to believe as a people that we don't need God, sometimes we're deceived to believe gradually that we don't need the church. We can say to ourselves that we have friends. We have family. We have all kinds of entertainment. The church used to be the social center of the community as well as the religious center. The church isn't the social center anymore. And sometimes we believe or get the feeling that we don't need the church anymore. And yet, I would remind us this morning that we need love. We need to know that someone cares about us. We need to know that there is something about our lives that is important.

Not something that we have done, but something that God has done. And oh, how we need the fellowship of the church to bind us together in the spirit of love. To strengthen each other, to encourage each other in the world where there are so many pressures and so many people expecting us to accomplish so much. How we need fellowship to tell us that it is all right just to be as you are, a child of God - loved and accepted. And let his strength and his wisdom to come as our guide.

And how we need the church as the guidance that it gives to us through his word. For us we go out into the world we find so many things that will lead us in so many directions that we begin to ask the question, "Which way is his light? Which way is life where there is meaning and joy and happiness and fullness of life?"

And so, the church stands as the one to nurture and guide and strengthen us through God's word. And is no other generation needed the church – we need the church. But it is so easy for us to gradually feel that we don't need the church.

Or sometimes there is the flipside of it. The gradual feeling comes that the church doesn't need me. And that is a sad day, isn't it? Yet so many people reach that day of feeling that the church really doesn't need me. And so, we begin to not attend. Or not attend and not serve. Or not attend and not serve and not give. And just begin to float along as if somehow the church doesn't care what happens to me. That is a gradual feeling.

Every now and then I run into someone who down the road of life has veered off of their path to say, "The church didn't need me, so I didn't go back." Let's stop and look for a moment and ask the question, "Is this the deceptive feeling that has come upon us gradually?" For the church needs every person that it can marshall this day to render our witness in the world. To say that Christ has come to give us life. And to give us hope. And to guide us down the pathway of life for as we stop and we look at what is happening in our land. And we call ourselves a Christian nation. We use that term loosely.

The crime rate is standing at an all-time high in our city. Did you know that it is safer to walk the streets of New York than it is in Mobile, Alabama today. That's a startling and alarming fact. We have one of the highest crime rates in America. Three times higher than many metropolitan areas twice our size.

And you say, "The church doesn't need me." We have one of the largest drug problems in our society located here in our own area. Wrecking the lives of countless people. God is calling for us to be the ministering body of Christ to his people. And for us to say that the church doesn't need us, we have been deceived by the gradual moving of ourselves away from his call and his challenge to be his body in this world.

The prisons are full. We have just voted a new bond issue to build more prisons because we don't know how to handle the people who are going down the wrong way. And to say that the church doesn't need me and doesn't need you is to be deceived with the process of gradually moving away a step at a time until finally we think the church doesn't need us and doesn't care about us.

And then fourthly, there is the deception of the gradual feeling that anything goes. It's all right. Little sins don't hurt. Little wrongdoings – "Everybody does them. I don't really need to stay in relationship to God. I really don't need to revive my heart and my mind and my soul and my spirit day by day. I can float through life. Anything goes."

That is one of the easiest feelings to come upon. When we stop and we look around we see that there are so many places that anything does go. And it is all right it seems. It seems as if they're making it as well as we're making it. It seems as if life is as good to them as it is to us. And so, we begin the process of saying, "It's all right." Little sins and mistakes and failings and little acts of selfishness and little self-centered attitudes can lead us down a way, "It's all right." That is the gradual feeling.

And yet, I would remind us that sin destroys us. I cannot hate without hate consuming me. I cannot lie except I become false. I cannot stop loving without becoming less lovable. The power of sin destroys the image of God in us. We might sometimes be led into the false security of believing that anything goes, but sin always leaves it' s mark. For God has called us to be his own.

And God has breathed into us the breath of life. God has given us a nature of love and opened to us the doorway of truth. And if we are ever to be the kind of children that God would have us be. If we are ever to experience the abundant way of life that Christ came to share with us, we have to be aware that sin always destroys.

The gradual is deceiving. It takes away the very meaning and the purpose and the joy of life if the gradual happens to be sin. And so, I would remind us this morning that there is a problem in allowing ourselves to drift complacently.

The passage of scripture that I read to you is from the book of Acts as Paul was crossing the Mediterranean Sea. The sailors became aware that drifting was very dangerous. The only reason they survived was that when they begin to realize that they were nearing the rocky shoal they cast out four anchors and prayed for day.For the next day the boat did break up. Because they ran aground.

We allow the gradual feeling that we don't need God. Or the gradual feeling that we don't need the church or the church doesn't need us or that anything goes. If we allow these gradual feelings to let us drift down the road of life, we are the loser. We are the ones that find ourselves broken upon the eternal laws of God.

Thank goodness, in God's economy there is the renewable. For there comes God's word to strengthen us and share with us his love. There comes the fellowship of the church to reach out with love and care and say, "We care what happens to you. We care that your life has meaning and purpose and joy and happiness."

There comes the hour of study. There comes the opportunity of meditation. Of being open and letting God's strength renew us again that we might not be deceived by the gradual but that we might keep a diligent watch of our faith. That we might be wise in the ways of life. That we might come to walk in the footsteps of the master, who shared with us the joy of eternal life.

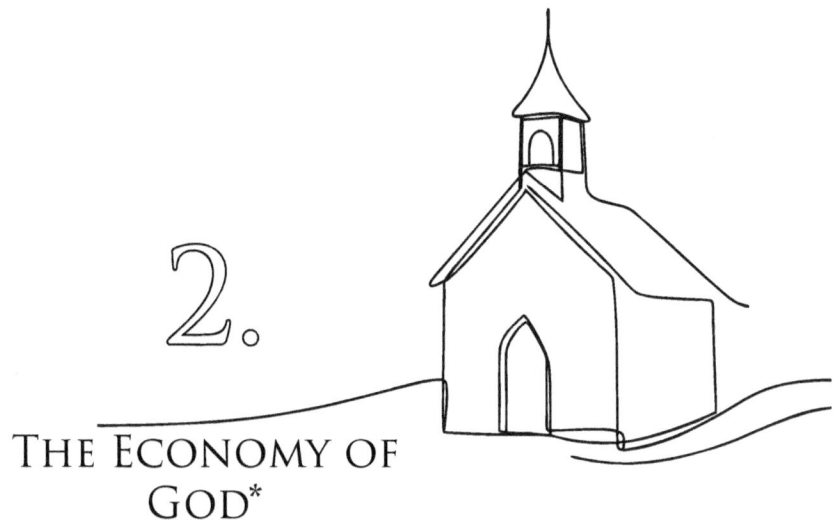

2.

THE ECONOMY OF GOD*

Matthew 13:31 – 32
He told them another parable: "The kingdom of heaven is like a mustard seed, which a man took and planted in his field. Though it is the smallest of all seeds, yet when it grows, it is the largest of garden plants and becomes a tree, so that the birds come and perch in its branches."

When I was but a lad in high school I was part of an organization called the FFA (Future Farmers of America). For those who were planning to go into farming, they encouraged us to grow various forms of livestock and one of the things they had was a pig chain. If you didn't have enough money to buy pig, they would buy a pig and give it to you. When your pig got big enough to have pigs then you would give back two pigs for the one you got. They called it returning in kind and with interest.

You know I think this says a great deal about God's economy too. The prophet Isaiah, second Isaiah, as he was writing to his people in captivity in Babylon was to remind them that God had blessed them and had made them a nation of priests. Now they were to be a blessing to all nations. God was blessing them not to keep that blessing but that that blessing might flow through all their lives to touch the lives of all of God's children. This is true in the life of Christians. God blesses us with his love and his care but he blesses us not only for our sake, but that we might be a blessing to those others. God does not call us to be receptacles of his grace but to be channels of his grace. When we think that we can receive God's love and God's grace and keep it to ourselves and hold it and not share it, we find a strange thing - that we always end up losing it. The only way we ever keep God's care is to give it away. And so we are to be channels, not receptacles, of his grace. He touches us with his love and with his care. That is why we are here this morning. We are here because he has touched us.

But there comes the second touch. What do we do with that second touch of love and grace and care that he has given to us? He is challenging us to touch others. That's the second touch. He touched us first. The question comes - have we let his grace flow through our lives to touch others? And so for a few moments this morning I would like for us to think together about the second touch. About the way that God would use us to touch the lives of others. What touch he would have us give them and what his touch has given us.

First of all, there is a touch of love. Jesus touched the lives of the disciples with the love. He touched them in such a magnificent fashion that it transformed them and turned them around. Before Jesus touched his life we see a soldier there - Simon the Zealot - committed to killing all the Romans that he could. His life was filled with bitterness and hate. Jesus touched him with love and transformed him. And then there was James and John. You know we think of John as a gentle and loving disciple. We read the gospel of John and it moves us to think about his nature. But they were known as sons of thunder because of their temper. Peter was a rough fisherman. Matthew was a tax collector. And on and on we could go. One after the other. And all of a sudden we see that when Jesus touched them it was a transforming and healing touch that made them new people. But he did not touch them with love for it to stop there. But he touched them with love to send them out. Even before he was crucified, he sent them out. You recall on one occasion that he sent them out to proclaim the Kingdom of God, to teach, to preach, to heal. He sent them out to touch others as they had been touched themselves.

The church came into existence and grew to magnificent fashion because the disciples were willing to be channels of God's love. They were willing to let the touch of love that had transformed their lives reach out and touch someone else.

For I think of a man like Albert Schweitzer. A man whose life was marked with brilliance. A brilliant mind, he had become a doctor of philosophy and a doctor of music. Then he felt the call of God to become a physician. He goes back to school again and becomes a medical doctor. So many places were open to him to minister to people there on the continent of Europe, but he said, "No, I want to go and touch the lives of people who are no one else would go." We see this brilliant man reaching out with a touch of love that God has touched him with, and he takes it to the heart of Africa and touches people whose lives have never been touched before in such a magnificent fashion.

We are here this morning because we are touched. God's word has touched your life and my life. God's son has touched your life and my life. God has used our parents, or our Sunday school teachers, or our minister, or a school teacher or a friend or someone to touch our lives. And we're here because of the touch of love. But the challenge is for us to go out and touch someone else.

You know sometimes we ought to think of the church gathered on Sunday morning as the football team in a huddle. We are here calling the play but the action begins when we walk out the door when we go out and begin to touch the heart and lives of those people who do not know God's love and care. God is calling for us to be the second touch. We have received the first, let's give it away to help someone know they are loved.

And there is the second touch that I see that Jesus gives us that he would have us share - that is a touch that is filled with healing. There are so many hearts in our world. There are so many people that live with hurts day to day. But you know the wonderful part about the Christian faith is that Christ comes to touch us not only with love but with the healing touch.

a

The first healing touch is the touch of forgiveness. When we've gone down the wrong road and done the wrong thing and we've hurt people and we've hurt ourselves and we stand at the point of needing to be brought back to God's loving care. The thing about Jesus Christ is that he touches us with forgiveness if we will let him. I think one of the most beautiful stories we find in the Gospels is in the last chapter of the Gospel of John where Simon Peter has denied Jesus three times, even when he is aware of the nature of the death that has been. There's nothing he can say. Then Jesus reaches out with a touch of healing. He forgives him. He doesn't say, "Because you have denied me three times, I'm not going to let you proclaim the Gospel." He said, "Do you love me? Feed my sheep."

All of us need the forgiveness of God. All of us need to be touched with that forgiveness that will set us free. To know the joy of living. And he touches us with it and he challenges us to pass it on. As we have been forgiven, learn to forgive others. You know, I don't know of anyone that ever experienced the touch of forgiveness that transformed their life more than John Wesley. When John Wesley could say that "My sins had been forgiven. Yeah, even mine." And the people and the leadership of England looked out and saw the ones who went to the mines and the factories day in and day out. They kind of marked them off and said these people don't count. But John Wesley was to touch them with the healing touch of God and the healing forgiveness of God.

And say that your life is important. That you can be forgiven and that you can be loved. That life can be good.

Or Martin Luther, a monk struggling in his cell to try to find some hope or peace in his own heart and mind. Day after day, week after week, and finally year after year. There seemed to be no cessation of the struggle of his soul. And then there came the touch of healing, of forgiveness. And he was to say that man is forgiven and shall live by grace alone. Not by the works that we do with our hands but by the unmerited love of God who has touched us with forgiveness.

And I would remind us as Christians that the world needs the touch of healing and the healing power of forgiveness. There are so many people who are dragging around the burdens, the sins ,and the stains of the past that Christ wants to forgive. He wants to make them whole and he can see you and me to be his second touch - the touch of forgiveness.

b

The second healing touch is not only the touch of forgiveness, but the touch of understanding. All of us want to be understood. We may not be right. We may do things wrong. We may hurt people. We still want to be understood. Jesus had a marvelous way of understanding, and in so doing, touching a person's life. He gave them the power to be healed of the sins that had encompassed their lives.

I think of the woman in the 8th chapter of the gospel of John who was taken in adultery. Here the Pharisees came and got their stones and they said the law says we should stone her. And Jesus began to talk to them about their own lives, about their sins and then he said, "He who is without sin cast the first stone." And one by one they left until Jesus was alone with the woman by himself. And Jesus said, "Where are your accusers?" And the woman said, "I have none, Master." He said, "Neither do I." Here, the only sinless man that ever lived said, "Neither do I." He understood. He would not stop there though, he said, "Go and sin no more," for he touched her with understanding and love, to heal the sin sickness of her life.

Or I like to think of a man like Matthew who was a tax collector. He was collecting taxes from his own countrymen to give to Rome. He was hated. He was despised. I don't know why Mathew was a tax collector. But Jesus saw something that was beneath that exterior of Matthew. That made him know that there was a heart that cried out for forgiveness and understanding. When everyone else walked by on the other side and had nothing to do with Matthew and didn't want him in their homes - the thought of this evil person. I see Jesus walk by that tax booth and stop. I see the shadow of Jesus fall across the stooped shoulders of the man with eyes cast down. I see Jesus looking down in love and understanding and he says. "Matthew. Matthew follow me." So all of a sudden Matthew found that someone did understand. He rose up, walked with Jesus from then on till the end of his life, gathering the sayings and teaching of Jesus to write for us one of the most comprehensive gospels we have. Because Jesus understood. And he touched him with understanding and healing and with forgiveness and with love. And Matthew became a new person.

All of us need to be understood. I don't think there is anything quite as lonely as to feel that no one understands how we feel, how we care. Thank goodness for the Christian faith. Jesus understands and touches us that way. He calls us to go out and touch others in the same fashion.

C

And then he touches us with direction. The way our life is headed. He touched the disciples and he said, "Follow me." God touched Amos and he said, "Go proclaim justice to my people." He touched Jonah and said, "Go proclaim the good news to the people of Nineveh." He touched Isaiah and Isaiah said, "Here am I. Send me." We all need the touch of direction. We all want our lives to count for something. To go in a direction that's meaningful, that's useful, that's helpful. And we need God's touch of direction. We need God sometimes to use someone else to touch our lives. To direct our lives.

I will forever be indebted to a teacher I had in high school. One day this man drove out from his office after school to sit down and talk with me. And he said, "I want you to do something for me - not that I don't think I can do it. I have faith in you. But do you have faith in yourself?" He touched me with a sense of direction I shall never forget because I needed it. All of us need to know that God is touching our lives and guiding us and that all of us need to pass it on. We need to pass that touch on to our children. You know that we guide our children in so many things. We guide them in what they should eat and what they should wear. What they should spend their money for. And sometimes we get real bashful about touching their lives and guiding them about following Jesus Christ. The most important thing in their world is to let God's love flow through their lives and cleanse them of their stains and set them free to live as God's children in this world. We need to guide them. We need to guide our children and our grandchildren and those we minister to and those that we touch. We need to touch them with guidance.

And then thirdly, not only has God touched our lives with love and he challenges us to touch others with love. Not only has he touched our lives with healing and challenged us to touch others with healing. But he has touched our lives with hope.

When the world reached its darkest era, God sent his son. God so loved the world and all of its frailty and all of its sin and all of its shortcomings. God so loved all of us that he sent his son that hope might be planted in our hearts. Jesus was to call himself the Prince of Peace that man might somehow learn to beat the instruments of war into the instruments of peace that we might dwell together as brothers and sisters of Christ Jesus. God touched us with hope. There is hope for our world today because of Jesus Christ. There isn't hope because of the energy we have or the power that we can produce or the number of people that are here but there's hope because the power of love can change our hearts. And can make us a people that can dwell together as God's children.

I would challenge us this morning to be a part of that hope through the life of the church. For the secular world stands in the sins of hopelessness. Not too long ago I read again the line of Bertrand Russell where he said, "The earth must be the insane asylum of this universe. For all the other planets have sent their people who could not adjust." And I thought oh so tragic. If he only knew Christ. If he only knew that God would take our twisted lives and make something beautiful out of it that our world can be a place of love and peace and harmony because Christ has been here. Because through his love we can transform the lives of those who don't yet know him. And I would point out also that touch of hope that God gave us was not only the touch of hope for the world but a personal touch. There is hope for my life and your life.

As I think of this I think of a man that I had the privilege of being his pastor a goodly number of years ago. The first time I saw him he was pretty much like most of us. Filled with a great deal of negative feeling. Everything was wrong. He didn't like people. He didn't like life and no one was fair to him. And he was always telling us how bad life was. But he started slipping in on the back row of the church and sitting there Sunday after Sunday. Part of the time because his wife made him come and part of the time because he wanted to come. His attitude began to change and then one beautiful Sunday morning as we were walking across plowed fields (he was a farmer) he stopped me and he said, "Preacher, you know this is a good world and this is a good life and God has been so good to me." And then he looked up and said, "I want to join the church in the morning, for God has changed my life." There is hope.

There is hope for our personal lives because Jesus Christ touched our lives. And there is hope to be shared because he would have us reach out and touch the lives of those who are near to us. We are here because someone has touched us. We are here because God has touched us. I would remind us this morning that God is calling us to be channels of his grace not receptacles of it, for he is challenging us to touch others until their life knows the joy of salvation.*

---

*   * From the only typed copy of this sermon that I could find that the indicated title is "The Little Things in Life" with referenced Bible verses of Matthew 13: 30-33. I changed the title and omitted the last verse referenced in the belief that doing so would better capture the intended topic of the sermon.

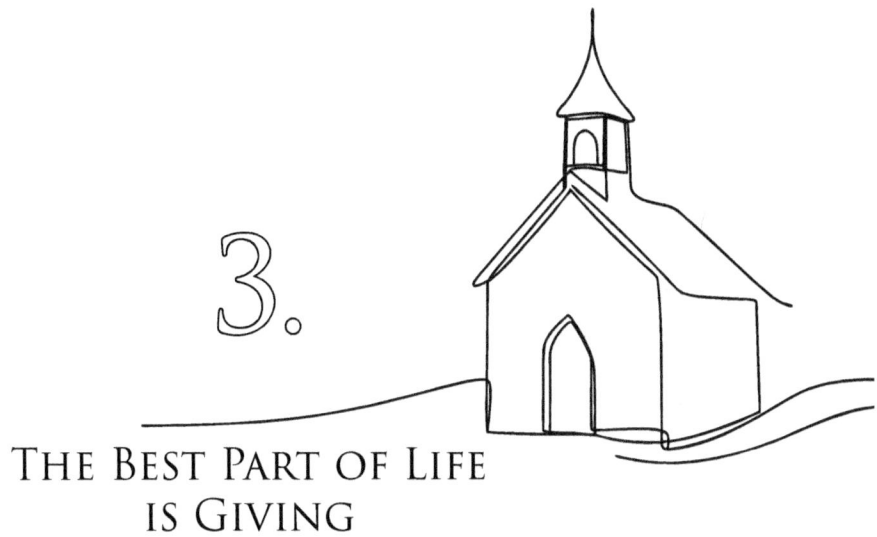

3.

THE BEST PART OF LIFE IS GIVING

2 Corinthians 9:6-10

Remember this: Whoever sows sparingly will also reap sparingly, and whoever sows generously will also reap generously. And God is able to bless you abundantly, so that in all things at all times, having all that you need, you will abound in every good work. As it is written: "They have freely scattered their gifts to the poor; their righteousness endures forever." Now he who supplies seed to the sower and bread for food will also supply and increase your store of seed and will enlarge the harvest of your righteousness.

We all want to get the most out of life that we can get. We hear the people in the advertising field remind us of this as they give us beer ads or car ads or cosmetic ads. They remind us that "we only go around once in life" and that we should experience the fullest extent of life that we can possibly experience.

You know one of the things that sometimes we are led to believe by our society is that the greatest joys of life come in receiving the things that people can give us or the things that we can buy and give to ourselves. But this is not quite the whole story, for the greatest joy and the most everlasting joy that we can experience in life is not in receiving but in giving. For the best part of life is giving.

For a few moments this morning I'd like for us to think about what giving can do to us and for us. As we begin to look at the concept of giving we see it as old as the beginning of life itself. For God gave his breath to man. He breathed into man the breath of life and in so giving God did not diminish himself. He enhanced himself. He began to share life not only with himself but with all of his creation and life began to multiply.

So, giving is old as man's beginning. The first dimension of giving that I would lift up for us this morning is that giving is a discipline that causes us to grow. Now in a little while some of us or some of you will flip on the TV and you'll begin to see a football game. You will begin to see athletes who have spent a great deal of time giving of themselves. They gave their time, their strength, and their minds. And those who gave completely, learned to work as a part of a team. And they learned something about themselves. They learned the abilities that they had. They learned what they could do if they work together as a unit. They begin to grow in their abilities and their understanding of life.

Or you can take a student. A student has to be willing to give himself to the task at hand that his mind might be stretched. He might learn what he had not learned before. That he might profit by what the professor would share with him or the teacher. It is only in the discipline of the giving one's attention that a student learns what is before him.

Or we might put it this way as a laborer. As we labor, only when we give ourselves to the task, do we grow. The labor that works halfheartedly never grows in skill or understanding or appreciation of his job. It is only when we give our total being do we learn to appreciate what we are doing. There are many unhappy people today who are working in the world because they have never given themselves to the task at hand.

And so is the same principle in the Christian faith. If we Christians are going to grow we have to learn to give. The first part of giving is the giving of our hearts and our minds and our souls to our Lord. There is a lovely hymn in our Cokesbury hymnal that reminds us that God asks us to give our hearts to Him. I know there are people in the world that say, "If I give my heart to Jesus then I might lose something of myself. I might cease being who I really am." That couldn't be further from the truth.

If the athlete says, "I'll be a better player if I don't give my time and my energy to the coach and the team" he is only fooling himself. If the student says, "I will not give my time to my studies or give my attention to my teacher" he is only fooling himself if he thinks he'll be a good student. The laborer who says, "I will not give my best to my job but I will do a good job is only fooling himself". And when a Christian says, "I will come to accept Jesus but I won't give him my heart. I won't let his spirit guide and mold and motivate me because I'll lose myself if I do" is only fooling himself. For you know we are made in God's image and only when we come to give him our hearts, our mind, our attention, our purpose in living, when we come and let his spirit guide us, only then is there a fulfillment in life. As long as we hold ourselves back, as long as we give God but the fragment -the crumbs of life- we never find our true nature.

I see so many people who are lonely and who have emptiness in their lives, not because they are not good people but because they have kept themselves back from God. They never learned to give him their hearts. They never learned to say "Here I am send me!" They never learned the fact that in the giving they learn a discipline that makes them stronger, better people.

You know to keep ourselves from God, the image of God in us dries up. It is but a little fragment of life but the more we give our hearts to him, the more we respond to him in love, the more we let him lead us, the more we become our true selves. The more we find life becoming more of a cohesive unit. The more we find that we are not fragmented and broken and pulled and tossed about an all directions. And so the giving of our hearts to him is a vital part of living. It is a discipline that causes us to grow strong.

I would remind us that stewardship is yet another dimension of our giving. The giving of what God has blessed our lives with. And through stewardship, our hearts and our minds and our lives grow strong and quite often the giving of our stewardship - the giving of the possessions that God has given us as we return a portion of it back to him - we grow strong in understanding how to use all that God has given us.

We are not stewards of 1/10th of what God has given us. We are stewards of 10/10ths. Everything that God has blessed our lives with - our time, our talent, our possessions - they are his. But he wants us to use part of these for our own benefit. He wants us to use part of these that life might be rich and enjoyable and meaningful to us.

Every now and then I run across someone who says, "You know, I don't believe in giving to the church. That is throwing away what I have." And yet, I find them throwing it away in so many ways that benefit them not at all. But when we learn to give to God as stewards, we learn to give all of life and then he gives back. We learn to manage wisely what he has given us.

Now the 9/10ths will not go as far as the 10/10ths but 9/10ths managed with God's guidance will go a lot farther than 10/10ths scattered to the winds without your thoughts or plans or preparations. I would remind you that we are stewards of all. God would want you to use the blessings he has given you. He also wants you to use a part of it extending his kingdom to reach out, to minister to the suffering halfway around the world. To begin the process of nurturing and teaching those in our own midst. He wants us to minister wherever there are needs. And the giving causes us to grow strong. Because through giving, through stewardship, we learn to manage what God has given us.

The second dimension of stewardship that I would like to lift up to you this morning is the fact that it not only causes us to grow strong - through the discipline of giving- our lives are filled with joy. Have you ever seen an athlete who has given it all he had? It didn't really matter sometimes if he won or lost or it was a draw. There was a sense of joy in his heart. "I played the game well. I did the best I could. I gave it all I had" and there was a joy and a happiness in his heart because he had used the abilities that he had.

Or the student who comes from the test who said, "I gave it all I had." Sometimes it might be a C and sometimes it might be a hundred, but the important thing was that there comes a joy, because we give it all we have. Or the laborer who looks at the task that he is just completed. He has disciplined his life to give his energy, his thoughts, his plans, his dreams. He stops and looks at the task that he has just completed. It might not be a task that would thrill your heart or my heart but it thrills his because he knows he has given himself. And that is the way life should be. For when we give of ourselves there comes a joy. There comes a joy that no person or no event can take away from us. And so it is true in our Christian living when we give our hearts to Jesus Christ. When we as Christians have labored in love and in the midst of other Christians and in the midst of the world of need sometimes the world is not going to pat us on the back and say, "You have done a good job." Sometimes the world is going to ignore the efforts that we have done as Christians, but that is not the important thing. When you have given yourselves completely to God. When you have let his Spirit guide your heart and his wisdom guide your mind and you have been open to him there comes a joy that the world cannot ever take away from you. A joy that comes from God because you have given of yourself completely.

As I look back over a period of years and I think how many times the richness of life and the joys of life have come to those that I have had the privilege of being a part of their lives - as I have become a part of your life as your pastor. To watch a person give of themselves in a task of Christ-like love and sharing, we know that giving is the best part of life.

When we see that we have given hope to a person who is lost and they have found a new road of life that leads to triumphant living, your giving of yourself is the highest joy you can know. When you have seen someone hungry or ragged or someone sick and because of the giving of your time and your talent and your love and your possessions that you have seen them nurtured to health again, then in the giving of yourself there comes a joy that is surpassed by nothing else.

Sometimes when we come in the hour of worship and we kneel at the chancel rail of the church and we look up at the cross then we know that day, that month or that year we have given ourselves in his service who loves us and called us to be his own. There is nothing in life that can surpass it, for we know the joy of giving the life that God has given us.

The same as true of a Christian steward. Sometimes we hear the reports coming back from around the world of God's working in a place that we have never heard of before. Where darkened minds have been illumined by the light of his truth and darkened hearts have been illumined by his love we can say to ourselves, "Through God's grace I have been a part of that." Or when we think of what is happening in the inner city, in our own city, and we know that lights are being turned on for children who have no light except the light of the church.

We can say, "I'm a part of that through God's grace" that is a joy that the world can never take from us. And I see your faces every Christmas season when we go about the task of raising money for the Children's Home and we think of five or six or seven hundred children across the state who have no one else to love them but the church. And I see us reach the goal that we have set for ourselves and I see the joy in your hearts and lives.

When Paul was writing to the church at Corinth he was saying, "He that sows sparingly, reaps sparingly. The church that sows with an attitude of bountifulness reaps bountifully." I see it in your faces and your hearts when you have shared what God has shared with you.

Lastly, I would remind you that the best part of living is giving, not because it causes us to grow strong alone or not only because of the joy in our hearts but also because it makes us effective people. The athlete who gives himself completely to the task of becoming a part of the team becomes effective. The student who uses his mind and listens to his professors and studies his books becomes an effective student. The laborer who uses the skills that are at his disposal to do the task at hand becomes a skilled laborer. And the Christian who gives his heart to Christ Jesus and who knows the joys of serving and giving and sharing and becoming a part of the body of Christ here on earth can also know the effectiveness that comes through giving. For God takes our efforts and God takes our dollars and our cents and through the miracle of only his love he begins the process of multiplying what we have given. Give a good deed today in the spirit of God and he will multiply it. For as you give it to one, he shares it with another.

The same thing is true of our stewardship. As we let God's Spirit guide us. As we open our eyes to the ministry at hand. As we begin to see how he would have us use all of our possessions, not just a little portion of them, then we begin to see that God can effectively take and use it to train the hearts and minds of those in our midst and to those that we will never see until one day. Until one day every knee before Him shall bow and every tongue confess that Jesus Christ is Lord and Savior.

We are about the task of working in God's vineyard. Paul would remind us that if we work with sparing gifts of time and talents and possessions - we have a meager harvest. But if we open our hearts to him. Give of ourselves. Share with him our talents. Share with him our time. Share with him our concern. Share with him the blessings that he has blessed us with - then the harvest will be bountiful. The kind of church, the kind of world, the kind of environment that you want for your children and grandchildren - a Christian way of life - can begin to happen when we give of ourselves to the Lord, who gave Himself for us.

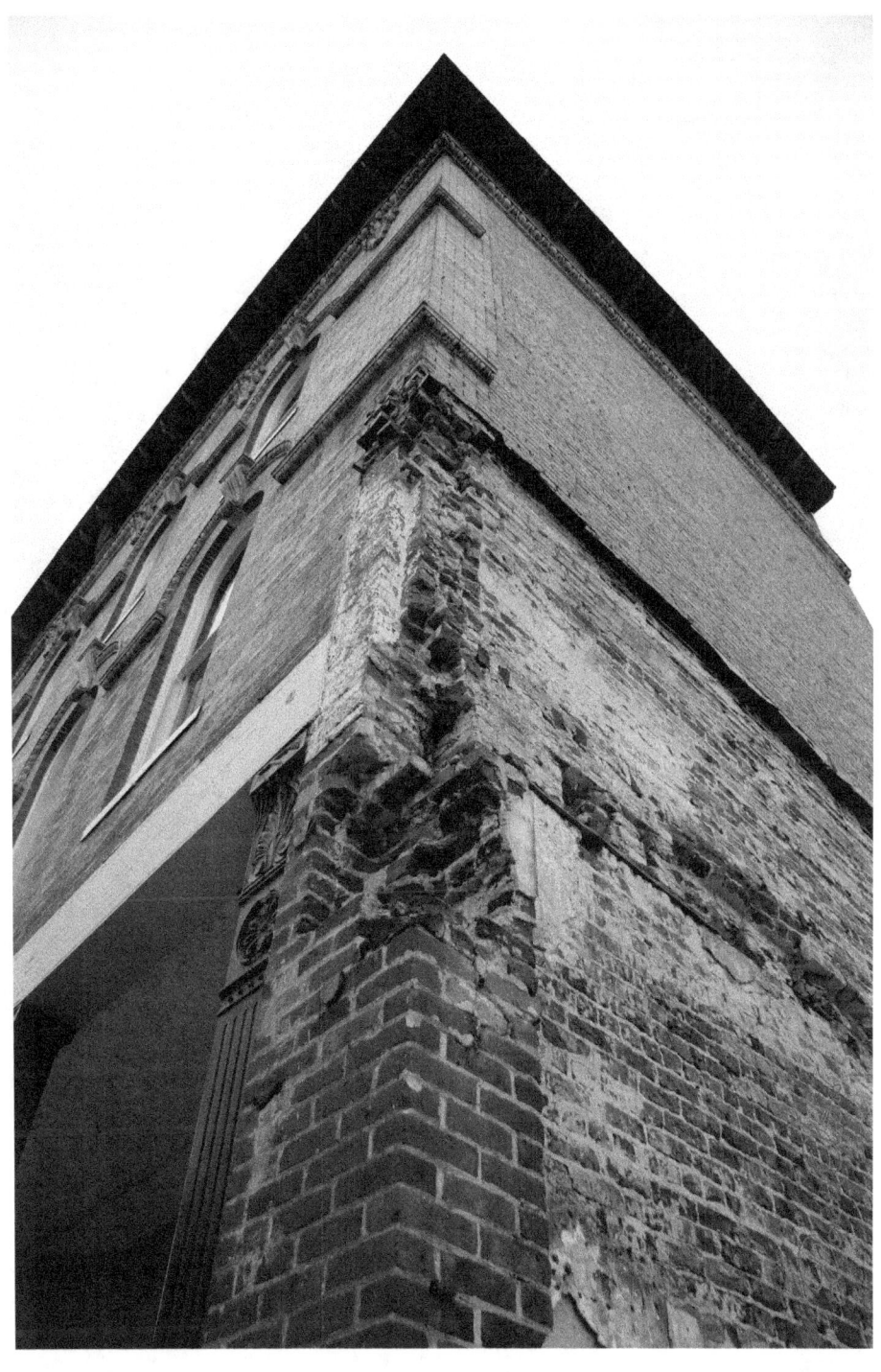

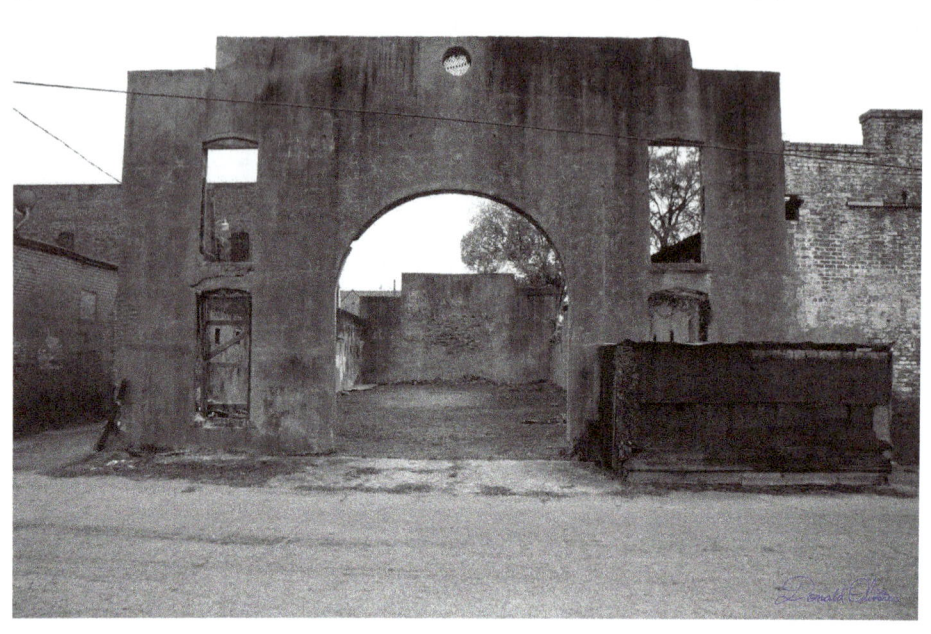

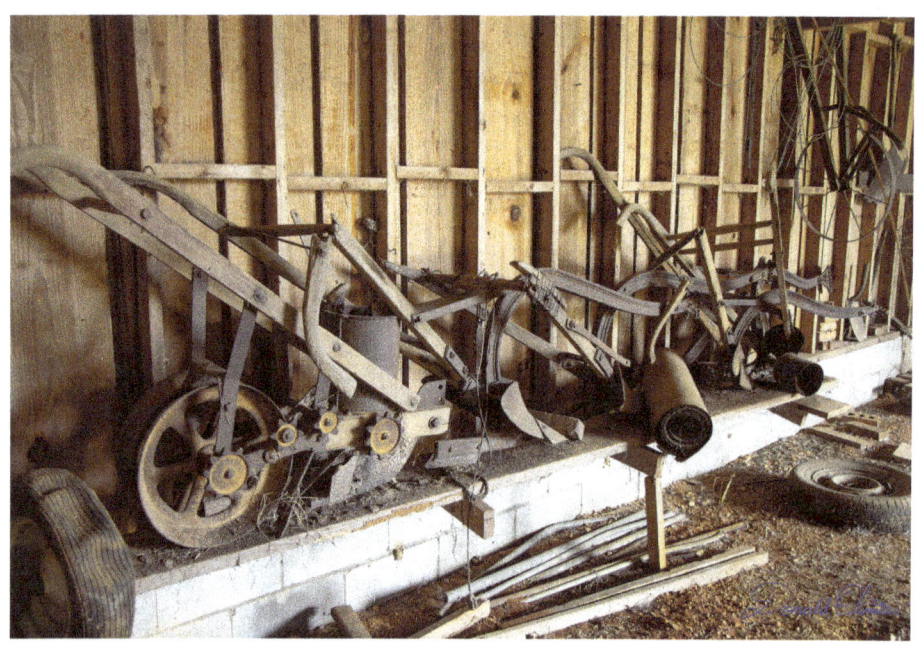

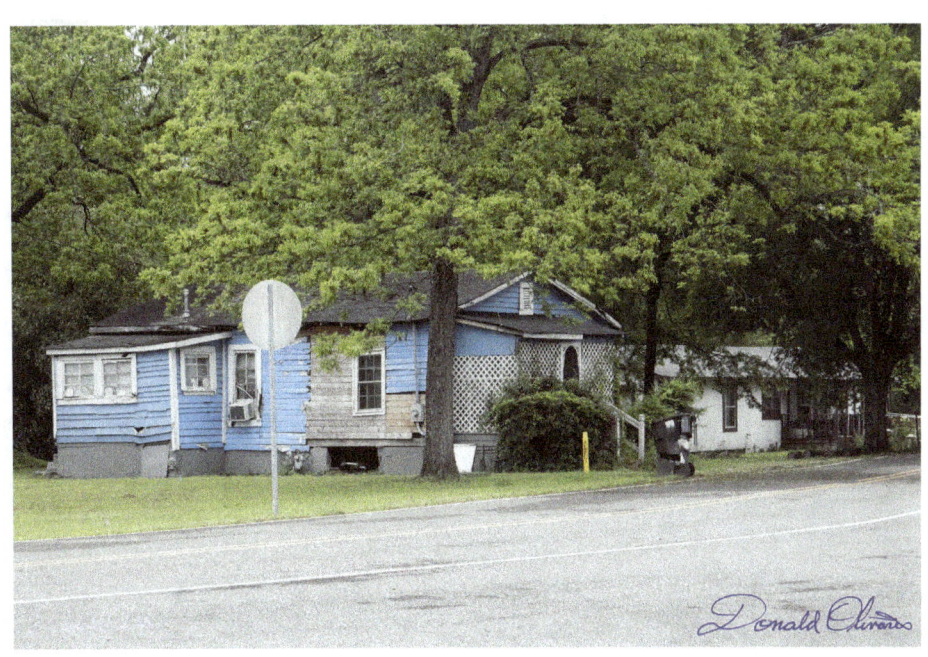

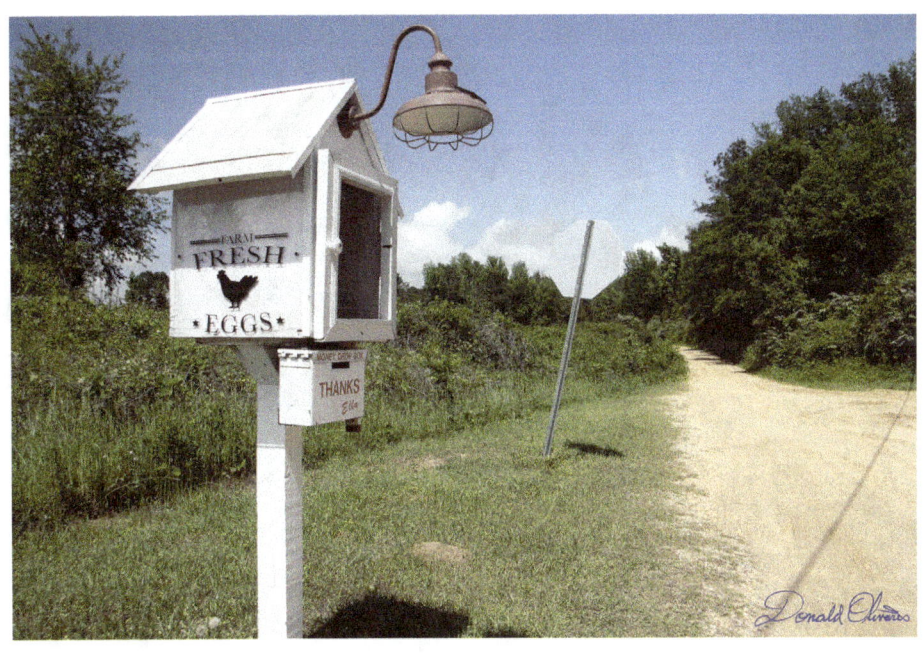

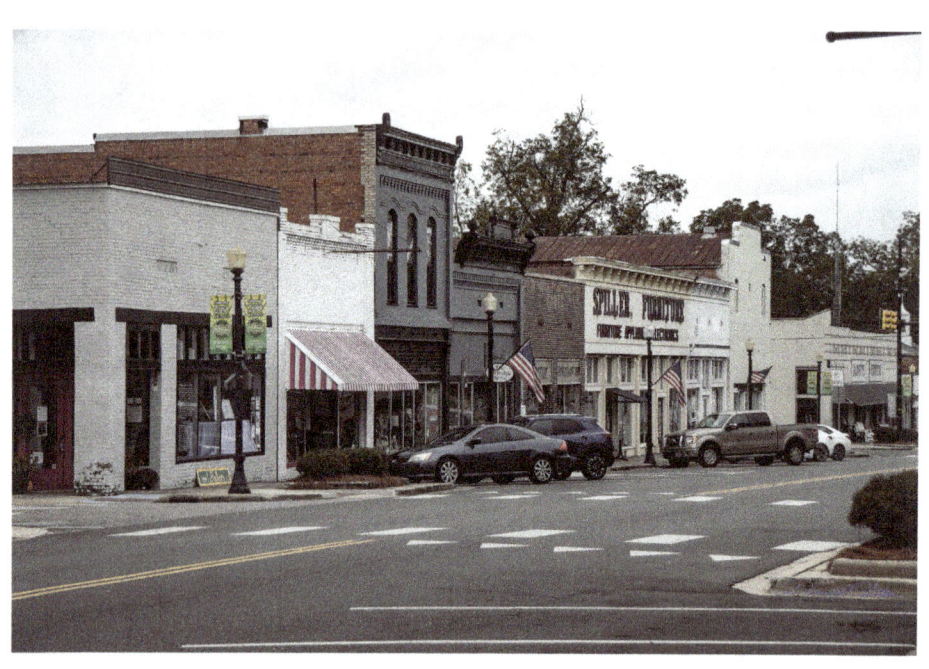

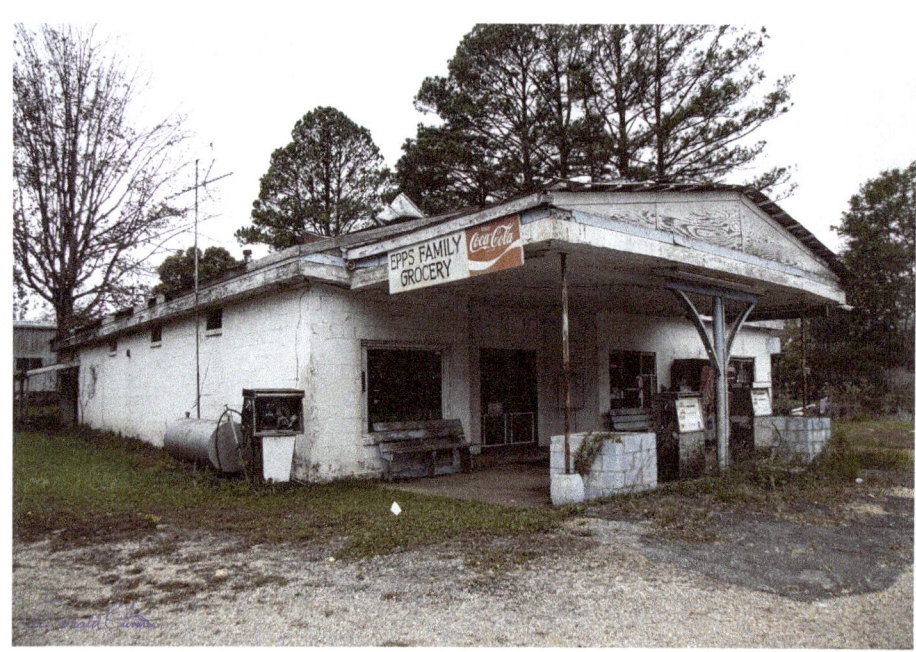

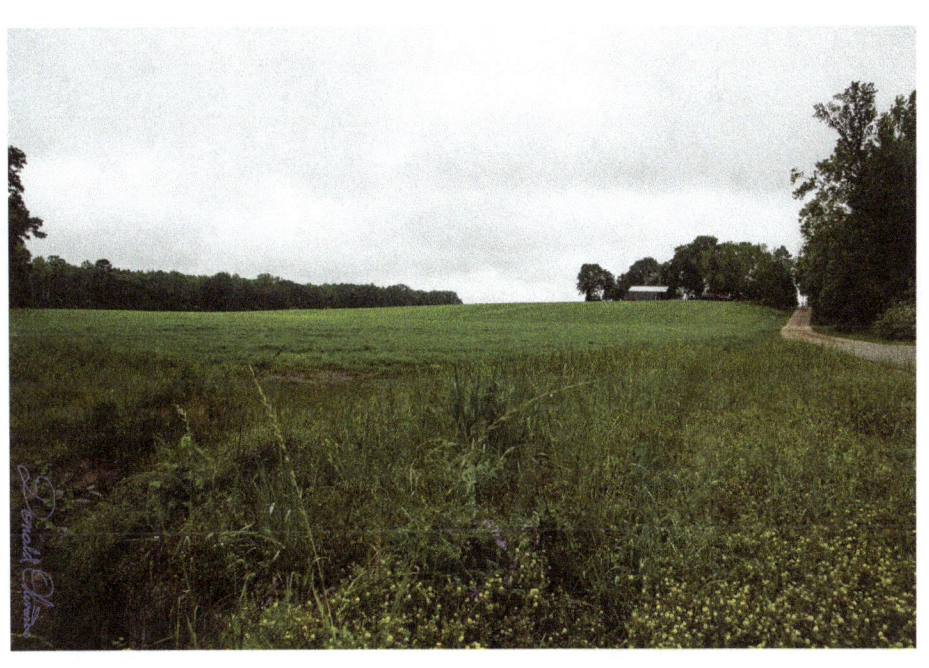

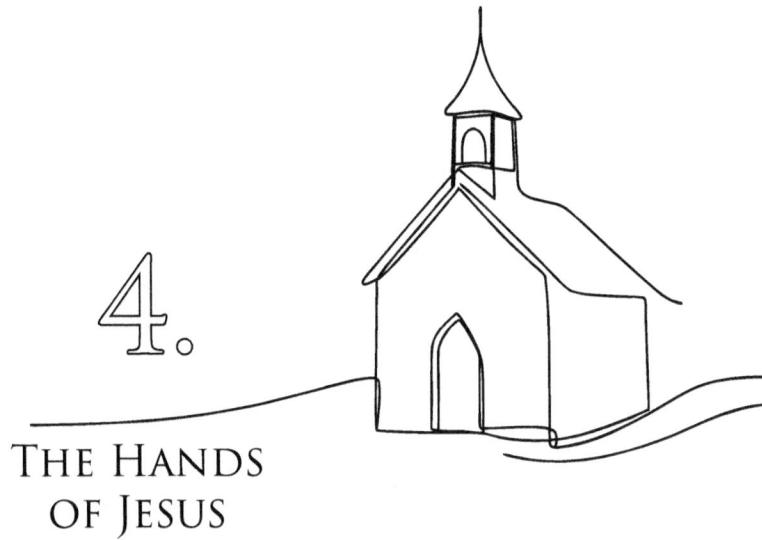

4.

THE HANDS OF JESUS

John 20:19-29

On the evening of that first day of the week, when the disciples were together, with the doors locked for fear of the Jewish leaders, Jesus came and stood among them and said, "Peace be with you!" After he said this, he showed them his hands and side. The disciples were overjoyed when they saw the Lord. Again Jesus said, "Peace be with you! As the Father has sent me, I am sending you." And with that he breathed on them and said, "Receive the Holy Spirit. If you forgive anyone's sins, their sins are forgiven; if you do not forgive them, they are not forgiven." Now Thomas (also known as Didymus), one of the Twelve, was not with the disciples when Jesus came. So the other disciples told him, "We have seen the Lord!" But he said to them, "Unless I see the nail marks in his hands and put my finger where the nails were, and put my hand into his side, I will not believe." A week later his disciples were in the house again, and Thomas was with them. Though the doors were locked, Jesus came and stood among them and said, "Peace be with you!" Then he said to Thomas, "Put your finger here;

see my hands. Reach out your hand and put it into my side. Stop doubting and believe." Thomas said to him, "My Lord and my God!" Then Jesus told him, "Because you have seen me, you have believed; blessed are those who have not seen and yet have believed."

Tomorrow is Labor Day. A day we set apart to recognize the importance of labor. Our hands tell a great deal about the kind of labor that we perform. Our hands also tell a great deal about the kind of person we are.

One of the first things that Jesus did after he rose from the dead was to show his hands to the disciples. Now Thomas wasn't in the Upper Room that night when Jesus appeared to them the first time. When Thomas heard them say that Jesus had risen from the dead, Thomas said, "Unless I see his hands - the nail prints in his hands - I won't believe."

For a few moments this morning I would like for us to think together about the hands of our Lord Jesus Christ. Of what they can say to us. What we can learn from them. And maybe we can learn something of how he would have us use our hands this day as well.

I think the first thing that we see, as that we begin the study of the hands of our Lord, is the fact that they were hands of a man who did manual labor. Jesus was the son of a carpenter. And I can imagine that at a very early age Jesus became a part of the work in the carpentry shop. At first, it might have been the kind of work that a little boy does as he learns to make believe or pretend that one day he'll be a carpenter. That one day he'll follow in his father's footsteps.

And I can imagine then not too many years later this young man could turn a piece of rough wood into something of beauty, into something of service. What we have in the Bible about the history of Jesus is very sketchy. We know that when Jesus was 12 years of age that Joseph and Mary took him to the temple. Past that point Joseph is never mentioned again and so I think that we can safely assume that Joseph died before Jesus begins his ministry.

Whenever Joseph died, the hands of our Lord not only were the hands that were learning to make something a beauty from a rough object, they began to be the hands of a breadwinner. Jesus being the oldest son in the family had the responsibility of providing for his mother and his brothers and sisters until they could provide for themselves. The task of being a breadwinner, of looking after his family didn't even end when Jesus was hanging on the cross. For the hands that it provided for his mother – as those hands were hanging from the cross – he was to say to his disciple that he loved, "Behold your mother."

It was a way of saying to John, "Take care of my mother. These hands can no longer provide for her the things that she will need, but your hands can."

Somehow as we see first of all that Jesus was a man who use his hands for manual labor, I think there are two lessons that we can learn from that picture. One is that no work that is helpful to mankind is demeaning. No labor that we can provide with our hands that is helpful for mankind is demeaning to us. The second is all of us need to learn to use our hands in some fashion for physical labor. For it is a kind of therapy, a kind of healing of the heart and the mind and the soul. Many times, when our minds and our hearts are filled with frustrations because of the day - the problems that the day has brought - it is so good that we can go out and dig in the yard and mow the grass or do something physical that has a way of draining down the tension.

We've come at a time in the history of our country when people tend to think that physical labor is not a blessing. I will try to reverse that thought as best I can. It matters not whether it is the washing of dishes or the cutting of grass or no matter how menial the task God has given us to do physical labor with, physical work so that the heart and the mind and the soul might find relaxation.

I'm sure there must have been many days when Jesus came from the carpenter's shop tired, but I'm sure also that he came very relaxed and happy with a sense of accomplishment. Because he had used his hands to make something. Used his hands to make life better for someone else.

Then I think there is a second thing that we can learn from the hands of Jesus. They were healing hands. Sprinkled all through the Gospel we found the stories of how Jesus touched people whose bodies were diseased and they were healed. He touched the blind eyes and they regained sight. Now we don't have the ability to perform such miraculous acts of touching the body and healing it or touching the eyes so that they can see. And yet, I would share with you that God has given many people the ability to have healing in their hands.

The doctors who touch a diseased body and through the skills that they have learned - the abilities that God has given them - can bring healing to a diseased body. Nurses can touch fevered brows and with love and knowledge can bring healing.

As I think of Jesus touching the eyes of the blind and they can see, I think of how we have doctors and many related professions in this field that give us the ability to see because as I look out over the congregation most of us, or at least a sizable percentage of us, need some aid to see clearly. What if we didn't have hands that make glasses? Many of us would miss a great portion of what we are now seeing.

Jesus had healing hands that could touch and make life whole. He has passed on to so many, the ability of touching and healing and enabling us to live life to its fullest if we use our hands as he would have us use them.

But there is another dimension of the healing hands of our Lord that all of us can be a part of. Jesus not only touched and healed the physical body but Jesus used his hands to heal the heart and the mind and the soul of those that he worked with. I think of the story of the disciples as they came into the Upper Room for the Last Supper.

There they were, filled with pride and arrogance because each one was saying, "I want to sit on the right or the left hand of the Lord when he comes into his kingly power." And not a single one of them would stop and do the menial task of washing the feet of their fellow disciples.

But, the hands of our Lord were not too good, for he stopped the meal, girded himself with a towel and went out and washed their feet one by one. And you know what happened - there was a spiritual healing. There was the healing of the heart and the mind and the soul of those who have been so filled with pride and arrogance. Now, as Jesus' hands were bathing their feet they could learn again that they were called to love and to serve.

Somehow as I was thinking of this, this week I began to think of how many times the brokenness of relationships have been healed by some good lady baking a cake or fixing a pot of vegetables and taking them to someone when they were in need.

Feelings may have been strained or resentment may have cropped up in one family to another but when somehow healing hands had come into the picture, God used your hands or their hands to bring healing in the process.

As I thought a little more, I thought how God can use us in such a simple way if we are willing to let him use us. That is usually the problem. We don't let him use our hands for the purpose that he has. I think of one parish that I was serving where there was a family that I visited. The man did not go to church at all. In fact, he not only did not go to the church, but he was very upset by preachers. They were the bane of his existence. He just despised to see the preacher coming. He would tell his wife that the preacher was the most worthless person that ever lived.

And his wife would say, "Now, preacher, would you pray for him? Would you come and talk to him?"

You know, I was wasting my time talking to that man. The more I talked to him the more he disliked me - the more he disliked preachers.

Finally, one day as I was thinking of a way to reach him, I realized that he needed some help and Saturday morning I got up and I put on my work shoes and my blue jeans and I said, "I can work with him for an hour."

That morning when I got there, we went out to the field and we plowed. I hadn't plowed in a goodly number of years, but it was a real relaxation to me. I didn't really do anything, but God took that and opened that man's heart.

I wonder how many times God has used your hands and my hands to bring about the healing of the heart and the mind and the soul of someone else. It doesn't take too much. It really doesn't if we let God use our hands. Jesus had healing hands it came to make us whole, not only our bodies but our minds and our spirits.

Then, thirdly I would remind us that the hands of Jesus were not only the hands of a manual laborer who knew the task of turning a rough piece of wood into something of beauty or the healing hands that made life whole for us, but Jesus also use his hands as loving and helping hands.

One of the loveliest stories in the New Testament is when Jesus took the little children up into his arms and he touched them. Have you ever thought how much it means to have the hand of someone that you care about reach out and touch you?

The disciples were so worried that Jesus would spend his time and his energy with these little ones that it wouldn't make any difference. But they were so wrong. Jesus took the time to let his hands touch those that needed to know that they were cared for. To touch those that were helpless that they might know that there was someone strong and someone who cared and someone who loved.

Also, I would say that the hands of Jesus, as loving hands, were seen another time in the Bible. Recall the story of the lady who was taken in adultery. There were those who wanted to stone her. Their hands reached out eagerly to grab the stones to end the life of one that they didn't approve of what she did. But Jesus had loving and helping hands. The only time we have recorded in the Bible where Jesus wrote, he took his finger and he wrote in the sand something. It was something that touched the hearts of all those people there in some fashion.

God gives us loving hands too. We can reach out and touch someone else that needs us to touch them. We can reach out with our hands and hold them up and strengthen them in the times of difficulty. We can reach out with hands of joy and love to share with them the beauty of life.

Then lastly, I would share with you the hands of our Lord we're not only working man's hands and hands that healed and hands that show loved but they were hands that revealed suffering.

When Thomas said, "I want to see the hands of our Lord." He didn't say, "I want to see the smooth hands of someone." He said, "I want to see the hands that have nail prints in them." Hands that have been so faithful to the calling of God and in tune with the needs of man that the object - the goal of life - was not to be stopped even if a cross lay in the pathway. So, Thomas said, "I want to see his hands - the nail prints there."

Jesus' hand showed the suffering that comes through love. I suppose if we thought for a few moments most of all of us could reflect and think of someone or a goodly number of people. Maybe our mother or our father or someone who is very close to us whose hands have become the symbols of suffering for us. For the labored long after the time of quitting should be, so that we might go to school. That we might have the opportunities that they did not have.

If we live long in this life and reach out to serve as God would have us serve, every Christian's hands will have some marks of suffering. For hat is one way we find relationship with our Lord. He counted no price too high to reach out and touch us with his love.

May the hands that led him to the cross be the hands that lead us to triumphant living.

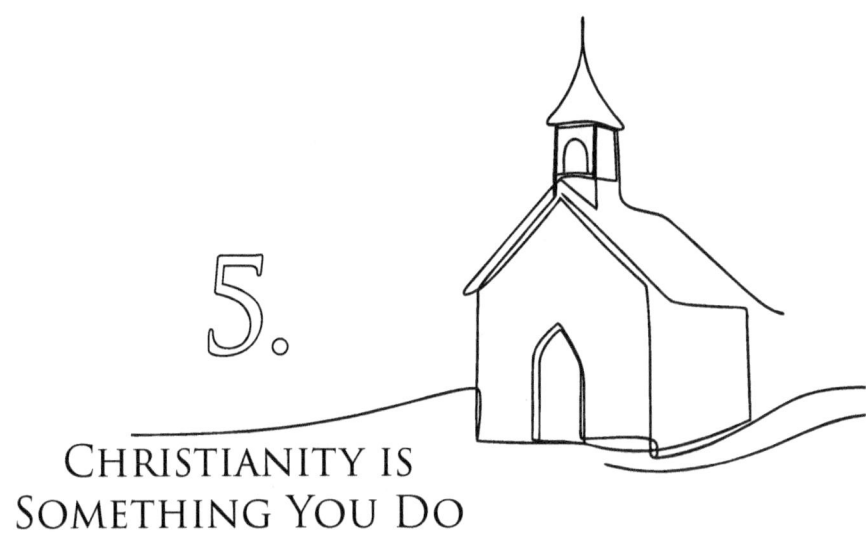

5.

CHRISTIANITY IS SOMETHING YOU DO

Matthew 7: 21-25 (RSV)

"Not everyone who says to me, 'Lord, Lord,' shall enter the kingdom of heaven, but he who does the will of my Father who is in heaven. On that day many will say to me, 'Lord, Lord, did we not prophesy in your name, and cast out demons in your name, and do many mighty works in your name?' And then will I declare to them, 'I never knew you; depart from me, you evil-doers.'"Everyone then who hears these words of mine and does them will be like a wise man who built his house upon the rock; and the rain fell, and the floods came, and the winds blew and beat upon that house, but it did not fall, because it had been founded on the rock. And everyone who hears these words of mine and does not do them will be like a foolish man who built his house upon the sand; and the rain fell, and the floods came, and the winds blew and beat against that house, and it fell; and great was the fall of it."

James 1:22-27 (RSV)

But be doers of the word, and not hearers only, deceiving yourselves. For if anyone is a hearer of the word and not a doer, he is like a man who observes his natural face in a mirror; for he observes himself and goes away and at once forgets what he was like. But he who looks into the perfect law, the law of liberty, and perseveres, being no hearer that forgets but a doer that acts, he shall be blessed in his doing. If anyone thinks he is religious and does not bridle his tongue but deceives his heart, this man's religion is vain. Religion that is pure and undefiled before God and the Father is this: to visit orphans and widows in their affliction, and to keep oneself unstained from the world.

The people who talked about being religious but did not act accordingly drew the sharpest criticism from our Lord. Jesus, himself, was a man of action. He worked. He healed. He fed. He ministered to people wherever he found them in need.

And so it is no small wonder that we find, both in the words of Jesus and in the words of James, a reminder that religion is something we do. Not something we say. As we look at James' understanding of religion, he was to remind us that there are several things that we are to do if we are to be what God would have us be.

First of all a Christian person, James was to say, would bridle his tongue. James was reminding the people that one cannot speak evil and good and be Christlike. One can speak good and be Christlike but if one speaks evil one is not Christlike. He was to remind people of how their words and their actions touched and affected other people.

I chose to read from the Revised Standard Version this morning because it shared with us a description of how one controls one's tongue that is meaningful to me. The term bridal means to control - which the new English translation says literally: "One controls."

When I was but a lad on the farm, a bridal was something that you put on a mule to get him ready to work. And if you bridled the mule, then you could use his strength and his energy. He could do something productive for you.

I think in the same sense when James was speaking of bridling one's tongue he was saying that until Christ comes and controls our lives. Until he bridals us. Until he harnesses that which is useful to us, we are of no use to him. On the other hand, when we are willing to let Christ control, we begin to think of what we say and how we say it and how it will affect others. We begin to think, "Is this what Christ would have me say?" Then we can be useful to Christ in his kingdom.

As I think of this, I think of two people in my ministry that I have known. I think of one little church when I was on a circuit, and I preached at this church once a month. Once a month after the preaching service in the morning, we held the board meeting or committee meetings or whatever we needed to do and we made our plans for the next month. Then Sunday night we worshiped and had a good fellowship together.

I found out after I had been there a couple of months that it mattered not what we planned on Sunday afternoon - it all became messed up during the following week. They would call and say, "Preacher, now the plans that we made we can't do."

And I would ask, "How come we can't?"

I begin to hear the name of one person saying, "I don't want to do it that way."

So one day I said, "We need to incorporate this person's thoughts into what we are doing."

So, the next meeting we were planning the Thanksgiving service. As we were planning the Thanksgiving service I asked this person to attend – the one who always had the voice of saying, "We can't do it that way." Halfway through the meeting this person said, "I don't like to do it that way."

Everybody else was an agreement and finally last I asked her, "Why, if everyone else wants to do it this way, why do you want to do it differently?"

A very unhappy person said to me (this was the lady), "If I can't run it, then I'm going to ruin it. I am not going to let this program take place without doing it my way."

I thought, "What a waste of energy. What a waste of thought. What a waste of action." Blocking, because they had never learned to be a part of the whole.

In contrast to this I think of a lady who was a schoolteacher. She was given, not only the good students but the bad students. And as she began each course there were those that would come in and say, "I don't like the course. I won't learn. I'm a troublemaker." They would always tell this teacher because she was of such a sweet disposition.

And to them she would always reply, "Yes, you've had problems in the past but we are going to do better this time. We're going to learn more. It's going to be a better year."

And you know, the amazing thing is that things always happened the way she said it would. There were those students who seem to say, "I just will not learn." But when they saw that she loved them and cared for them and that she spoke kindly to them and that she was always concerned that they should do the best they could do - they had a way of responding.

I think James is trying to say something to us like this. God gave us a tongue to pray for people, to encourage people, to lift up the positive of life. And when we do anything less we are doing less than a child of God should do. All of us, as we look at ourselves, are aware that we need his correcting, cleansing and guiding influence here.

It is so easy. It's so easy to let our tongues and our actions run the wrong way, but if Christ bridals us - if we let Christ control us - it won't be long until we feel the pull of his hand saying, "Not this way, son. Not this way, daughter. But pray, but lift up, but encourage, work in love." That is what James was saying to us.

And then there was the second thing that he was saying to us. He said that if we are going to be a Christian person, not only must we bridle our tongues and our actions that they might be useful for God's kingdom, but also he is saying that a Christian person will have a burning desire to minister to the poor and needy of the world.

You know, as Christians sometimes we get awfully selfish. We begin to think about our soul's condition and our lives and we stop there. Christ was always looking out to see those that stood in need and he began the process of ministering to them.

Many times, when Jesus was tired or he was weary from labor, people came to him who needed his help. He ministered to them. You know the great Christian giants down through the centuries that we admire and respect and appreciate in the Christian faith are the ones that had a burning desire to minister to the needs of the people.

I think of General William Booth who founded the Salvation Army. A group of people that no one seem to want to minister to. He was quoted on one occasion as saying, "Surely the 9/10 of the people should have a way of affecting the lives of 1/10 that are in such desperate condition."

He was saying that somehow we, as Christians, ought to reach out with love and care and minister to the brokenness of life. Christianity is not something that we talk about. It is something we do.

James heard a lot of talking and that is why in his book he reminds us that we are called to be people of action. Jesus was a man of action and he ministered to people in need. And so, if we as Christians are to be what God would have us be in the last quarter of the 20th century he would have us be people who would bind up the brokenness of life. Not just the physical. Sometimes the brokenness of life is more mental than spiritual.

We should have a burning compassion to share with them the Good News that God loves us. And that in God there is the healing power of redemption. The brokenness of life need not stay when the healing power of Christ is available. The hunger of life need not be as long as the word of God can feed our hearts and minds and souls.

But, you know the world is not going to know that outside these four walls if we sit smugly, contently in our own world. For to be a Christian we are called to be people of action. Caring, ministering, loving, reaching out to the poor and the needy of our world.

Then thirdly, religion is something we, not only by bridling our tongue and caring for those who are in need, but to have a desire to know and do God's will. To have a burning desire to know and do the will of our heavenly Father.

Jesus, in the sermon on the mount, was confronted by some who were working but they were not working in the spirit of Christ. And so, he was to remind them that we as the body of Christ, we as God's people, must always be guided by God. For he was to remind them that the foundation of life must be His word.

You know, the foundation of our lives is our selfishness. We think of what we want and what is good for us and what we would enjoy doing and we say, "That is where life is."

Wrong! That is where we are. But life is where God is and ours is the task of knowing God's will, seeking for it and then doing it. Oh, sometimes we think that Christianity is something we can selfishly hold to ourselves. That we don't need to be a part of a fellowship that calls us into God's presence in the hour of worship. Sometimes we think that we know God's will by ourselves and stop there - without the fellowship of the church.

As I think of this, I think of Dr. Samuel Schumaker who told the story of an English minister who was visiting one cold winter afternoon. And as he knocked on the door of one of his parishioners, the man invited him in and after a few moments of conversation said, "Preacher, I won't be back at church because I have found that Christianity is something of an individual thing. I don't need to come to worship anymore. And therefore, I can know God's will and I can do it all by myself."

The preacher did not say a word, but as they were sitting in front of a roaring fire he took the tongs and reached out and grabbed one coal - bright, glowing red coal. And he put it on the hearth. It's sat there for a few moments, and it began to turn dark red, and then gray, and finally at last black. And it was cold.

And without saying another word the man got the message. He said, "Preacher, I'll be in church next Sunday." For you see, God is calling and telling us to do his will but we can't do this by ourselves. That is why we have a fellowship. That is why we have a church. We come together to worship that we might know his will and do his will in our world today. And when we separate ourselves, we find that we, like the ember, grow cold - with no power, no influence, no strength. Christianity is something that we do. We do it together. We worship together. We serve together. We pray together. We let God's corrective power transform us together as God's people.

Jesus was to remind us that we belong to a fellowship. We are called to know God's will and to do it.

And then lastly, religion is something that we do not only because we bridle our tongues and minister to those about us and seek to know God's will and follow it, James was to remind us that to be religious we are called to have a deep personal integrity. The term he used is "to remain unspotted by the world."

Now, James is not saying that Christianity does not have to be in tune with the world. Paul was cast in prison. Jesus died a criminal's death. So we could go down the list of those who followed our Lord faithfully. The world did not always agree with what they did. But what he was saying was that we have a personal code of ethics and integrity that the world cannot look at us and say, "He's not like the Master because his life is unbecoming of the Master."

That is the greatest condemnation that any Christian can ever have. When we allow our personal conduct to sink to a level that the world will look and say, "That is not like Jesus would live."

You know, one of the hardest things we ever do as Christians in our world today is to live like the Master lived. And yet, I would say to us that it is the only way that the world shall ever be converted. It is the only way that we can ever enjoy the richness and fullness and joy of being a Christian. We can't live in the world and be a part of the world and let the world guide us and be a Christian.

If we are going to be a Christian, then we have to let Christ guide us. Christ has to stand at the center of our lives. Challenging our thoughts, our words, our actions. Challenging us to follow him. Until one day, we can say with Paul of old, "For me, to live is Christ." For Paul had heard the challenge of Christ so many times in his life. He had heard the upward and onward call of Christ until finally at last his life had begun to bear the marks of Jesus.

Christianity is not something that we talk about but something we do. It is a way of life. It is the attitude we have in our hearts. It is the love that we let flow out to reach around and grasp the lives of others. And somehow if we forget that, it becomes empty and void. Oh, the world needs to see the church in action.

They've heard our words. They know what our Lord has said. They know how we are supposed to live. Oh, now the world needs to know that we can live as Christ calls us to live. To let his spirit guide our thoughts, our words, our actions until those thoughts and words and actions make a difference. Not only in our lives, but in the lives of those we touch.

And I would remind us that religion is not only action but religion - the Christian faith - is joy. As we come to let the spirit of

God guide and direct us there comes an inner peace, an inner joy. We live in a troubled world because there are too many who often who allow something other than Christ to guide our lives.

Christ is calling for us to be people of action. To live triumphantly and with joy in this world. That the joy and the faith and the hope that we have will become so contagious by our living that it will draw others to him.

Let us remember, that the Christian faith is not something that we talk about. It is a life that we live.

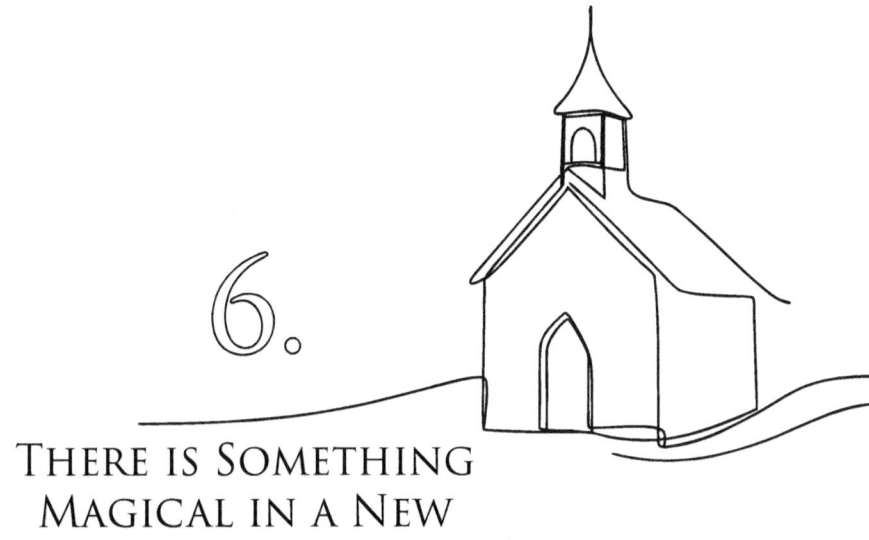

6.

THERE IS SOMETHING MAGICAL IN A NEW YEAR*

Philippians 3:12-14

Not that I have already obtained all this, or have already arrived at my goal, but I press on to take hold of that for which Christ Jesus took hold of me. Brothers and sisters, I do not consider myself yet to have taken hold of it. But one thing I do: Forgetting what is behind and straining toward what is ahead, I press on toward the goal to win the prize for which God has called me heavenward in Christ Jesus.

Today is the last day of December. Tomorrow we begin a new year. There is something magical about a new year. It is the beginning again. It is starting with a clean slate. Many millions of us will make resolutions. Resolving that the things that we did in the past year that were not right we will not do in the coming year. Or the things that we did not do that we should've done, we will do in the coming year.

There is one great problem with New Year's resolutions though. We have a way of forgetting them. We have a way of letting them slide. We have a way of losing that enthusiasm that we had as we begin to look at the things in our lives that need changing and resolved to change them.

So, this morning for a few moments I would like to think together about some of the ways that it will be helpful for us as we go into a new year to keep those resolutions that are good. Those resolutions that will make us better people.

First of all, I would say as we begin to make our resolutions we need to begin with God. For in our own strength, we fail. One of the reasons that we fail so often in resolutions is because that in our own light and our own wisdom and in our own strength, we will not do the things that we resolve to do. We find the nagging habits of the past pulling us back into old patterns. So we must start with God.

First we need to let his wisdom search us so that we can learn the things that really do need changing in our lives. One of the things that we have forgotten so often in the life of the church is that we need to stand or sit and quietly listen to God. To let him speak to us. When we pray we finish and we say, "Amen." We should wait a while in our own private thoughts to let his Spirit speak to us. To show us. To guide us that we might see the things that need changing.

We never will keep our New Year's resolutions until we are convinced that the things that we endeavor to do are things that we need to do. Until we see the need for change we can mouth the words. We can write on paper our resolutions, but they will never stick. They will never stay with us until we honestly face the fact that we need to change. And I don't know of a better place of facing that we need change than in the presence of God. Because he will guide us. He will nurture us and help us see those things that need changing in our lives.

Also, I would begin with God not only because he can help us see the things that need changing, but I would begin with God as I look at the things that do need changing in my life to let his love affirm me and affirm you.

That is something we need so desperately in our world today. To know that there is something of infinite worth in our lives. Not because we've put it there but because God has put it there. We are his child. We may be his child that stumbles. We may be his child that's fallen short of his glory. We may be his child that has gone away from him in selfishness. But we are still his child.

And when we begin with God, we begin again with the affirmation of the fact that we are loved. "For God so loved the world." Not just part of the world. Not just the people who are obedient. But God loves all of us. And as we begin to look at the new year and begin to resolve the things that we want to do and the kind of person that we want to be, we need to begin with God's love.

What does God want us to be? And how has his love surrounded us and nurtured us? For it is ever present. And then we need to let his wisdom or his hope encourage us. There are so many discouraging things that that happen in the world that sometimes we are tempted to become negative. We are tempted to look on the dark side of life. But I would remind us that in God's wisdom he made life good.

All of his creation he said was good. And he had a purpose and a plan for everything that he made. And so, as we begin looking at the things that need changing in our lives we need to begin to find the hope of God that the new year can be the best one that we have ever lived. And it can be if we go forth with God. If we begin with him. If we let his spirit search us and guide us. If we let his love affirm us and strengthen us. If we let his hope encourage us, then it can be.

And then, secondly, not only do we need to begin with God but we need to turn to him for our strength. It is not weakness on our part to turn to God but wisdom. God made us and he knows us. He understands us. And he would like to strengthen us.

When I say, "Trust God. Turn to him for our strength." I think of something not in the realm of religion but at the point of human weakness. Sometimes we feel like if we turn to someone for help it is a sign of weakness.

I used to have a friend who thought it was a weakness to go to a mechanic to get his car fixed. One day I was over at his place while he was working on his car. It wasn't running quite right. He was fully equipped, as he usually was. He had a hammer, and he had a pair of pliers and a battered old wrench. And you can imagine what happened as he began to work on his car. It began to run worse and worse and worse until finally at last it quit because he had worked on it too long.

The next day I saw someone towing his car down the road. Pulling it, because he had worked on it so long that he had jumped the timing. Now a mechanic knows what that is. All I know is that it won't start when that happens. And his wouldn't start.

So, on another occasion I was talking to him and I said, "Why don't you take your car to the garage when it stops running or when it gets in trouble?"

And he said, "That is a sign of weakness. I can figure out what's wrong. I can use my head and my tools, and I can make it run right." Then he looked at me and grinned and said, "I noticed that your car wasn't running too smoothly when you brought it up."

I said, "That is all right. I'm on my way home now!" I didn't want him to get a hand on my car. Because I knew what would happen if he did.

Sometimes we are this way about God. We don't think that we should turn to God for strength. But, he knows us. He loves us. He's made us. He knows the need in our lives. And how we need to begin by turning to him to let his wisdom guide us. And let his love sustain us. We need to turn to him in prayer and in the moments of meditation let his spirit of gentle, calming force enter our lives. How we need to read his word that it might lift us and encourage us and chastise us. How we need to come in the hour of worship and honor him. And let his presence strengthen us. For God wants us to be strong and happy and useful people in the coming year. But we don't have to do it by ourselves. That is glorious part about the Christian faith. For God will strengthen us if we open our lives to him.

Paul was to say on one occasion, "I can do all things" (but he didn't stop there like we are sometimes tempted to do) "through Christ that strengtheneth me". And so, if we make New Year's resolutions ourselves we are probably going to fail and we are going to fall. But if we make them with an openness to God and letting his spirit guide us. With a willingness to let his strength nurture us. The odds are that we will become more Christlike in the next year than we were in the last.

Another dimension of his strength is not only does he nurture us with his love and guide us with his wisdom, but we need to turn to him in strength so that his power of forgiveness will cleanse us. We don't need to drag our guilt and our failure of the last year into the next. We'll fail enough times in the future without borrowing the failures of the past and depressing ourselves.

God in his love will forgive. Will cleanse. Will restore. Will strengthen. God in his infinite love wants us to be the best that we can be. And we cannot be the best person that we possibly could be if we drag around the feeling of guilt and failure. And that is why he has forgiven us. He will forgive us. He will cleanse us from all the stains of the past that we might go out accepted, loved and forgiven.

And then thirdly, as we begin at our New Year's resolutions not only do we need to begin with God and turn to him for strength, but the third thing is that we need to have a plan. It is easy to resolve something and say, "I will be better next year than I was last year".

But unless there is a plan it usually falls by the wayside. Not long ago I heard our district superintendent tell of a church that decided that in the new year they would take in 300 new members. Well of course, I'm sure that must've excited him when he heard a church say, "We want to take in 300 new members." Because the church didn't even have 300 members and the church had been there about 30 years or more and it seemed as if it wasn't gaining much and it wasn't losing much. It was kind of on a standstill. And all of a sudden it said, "We are going to take in 300 more members next year than we've taken in in all these years before."

And then he asked the question, "What is your plan?"

There was total silence for there was no plan. They had just resolved to take in 300 members. Now you know the likelihood of their success was very slim. We can resolve that we will not miss a morning worship service. That we will not miss Sunday school. Or that we will be where the church needs us to be. But, if we don't have a plan, then our best thoughts get waylaid by old habits.

If we resolve that we are going to worship service every Sunday morning, then Saturday night we need to check and see if our shoes are shined. And if our suit is pressed or our dress is ready. And then we will need to set the alarm clock. And then we need to get up. Everything that we resolve to do next year needs to have a plan attached to it. For without a plan, we shall not accomplish it.

And so, as we begin to look at the things that need changing in our lives let us develop a plan too that will help us change. If we are seeing things that need to be done that we have never done before. Let's develop a plan of how to do them. And I know I've no better way than to begin with God and to turn to him in strength and let him strengthen us and then be open to guidance of his Spirit.

Then fourthly, I would say, at a new beginning: don't let the old habits defeat you. You know your old habits are so much stronger and my old habits are so much stronger than our new resolve. If we resolve to do something it is evident that we haven't been doing it or we haven't been doing it the right way. And how easy it is in a little while to let the old pattern reach out and grab us and pull us down again.

I mentioned a moment ago about resolving to be at church every Sunday morning. I've had people tell me so often, "I was planning to come but I forgot to set the alarm clock." or "I was so used to sleeping that I just reached over and turned it off."

An old habit. Old habits have a way of sucking us back to the old way of life. But, if we know the old things of life we're not beneficial to us we need to have our souls on guard. We need to have our eyes focused on the fact that the temptations will come. And if we are aware that the temptations of the old patterns will come, then maybe we will be ready for them. If we open our minds and our hearts to new truths.

And then, lastly, new beginnings not only need to begin with God and feel his strength in our lives, to have a plan and to be aware of the old habits that would defeat us, but we need to learn to keep our eye on two things: the source of our power and the goal that we are trying to achieve. The source of our power is God. We Christians should know this best of all. That it is God's strength that enables us to accomplish anything.

And so, if we learn to keep our eye on God then we can march triumphally into the new year. And if we keep our eye on the goal of being God's person, of letting God's Spirit live in our hearts and minds then if we keep our eye on the God those goals can be accomplished.

The new year is tomorrow. New Year's Day it is a great and magical thing, but it takes a lot of hard work to translate the resolutions that we make into the kind of life that we should live. Let us resolve to let God strengthen and direct us and use our own minds and hearts to develop a plan. To use his wisdom and his love to make us the kind of people that he would have us be.*

* The original title of this sermon is "New Beginnings." It was changed because there is another sermon in this book with the same title. The sermon was delivered on 31 December 1978; all references to the specific year were removed.

---

*   The original title of this sermon is "New Beginnings." It was changed because there is another sermon in this book with the same title. The sermon was delivered on 31 December 1978; all references to the specific year were removed.

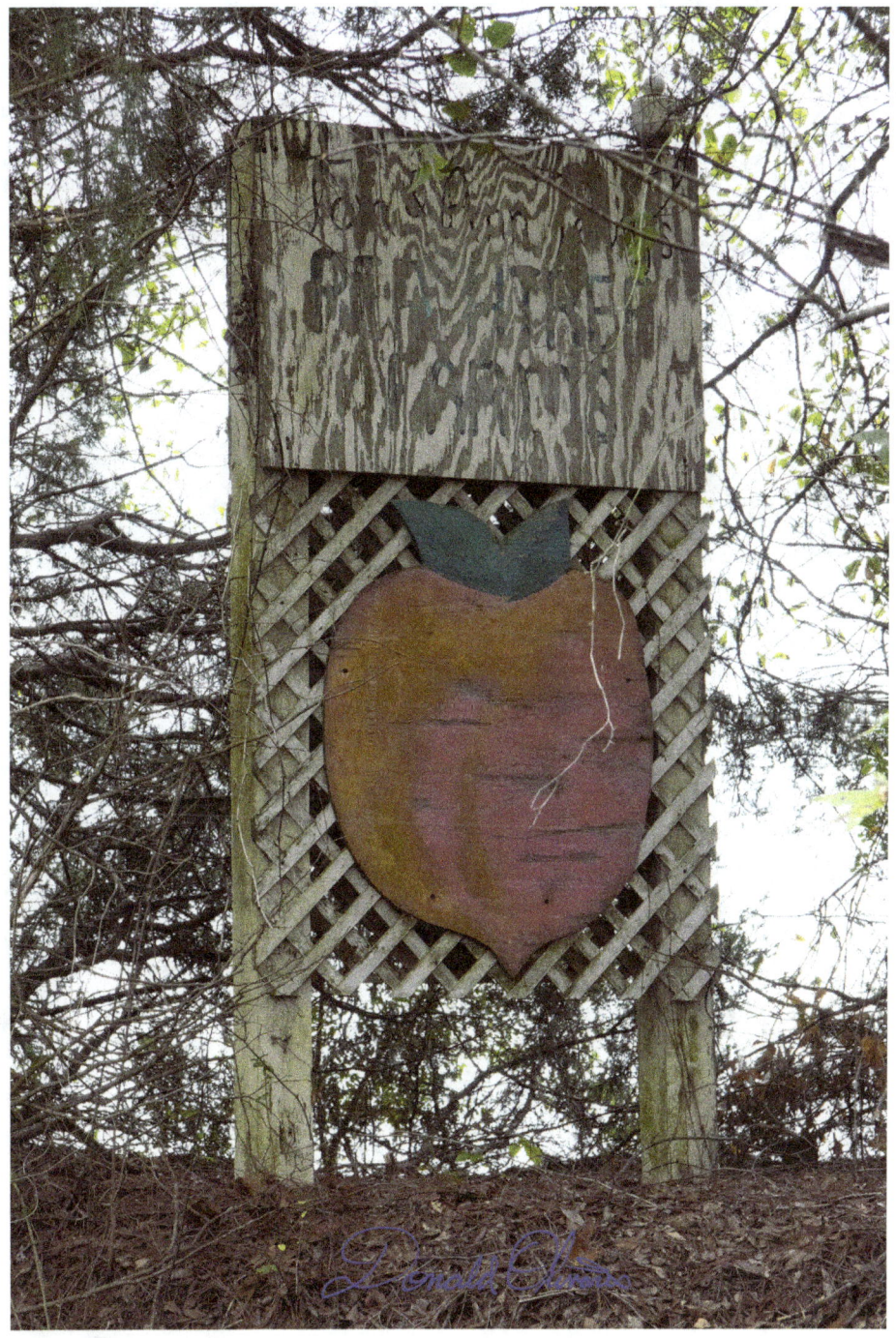

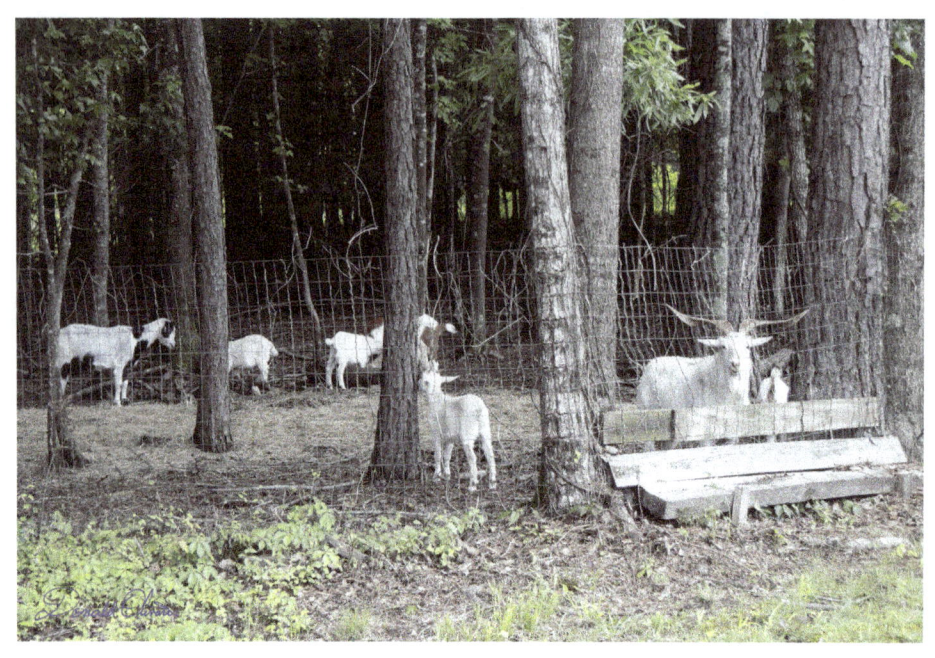

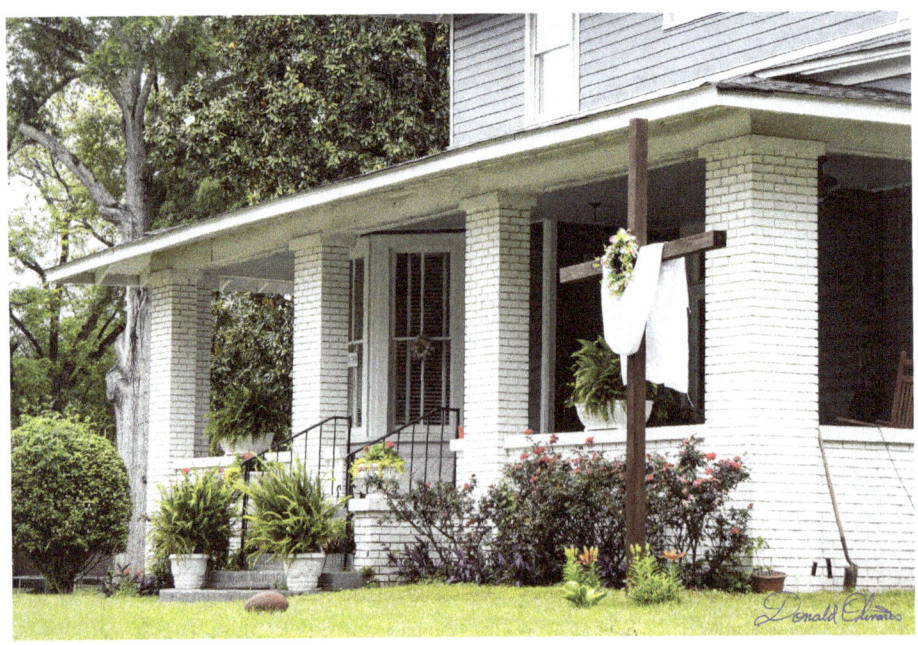

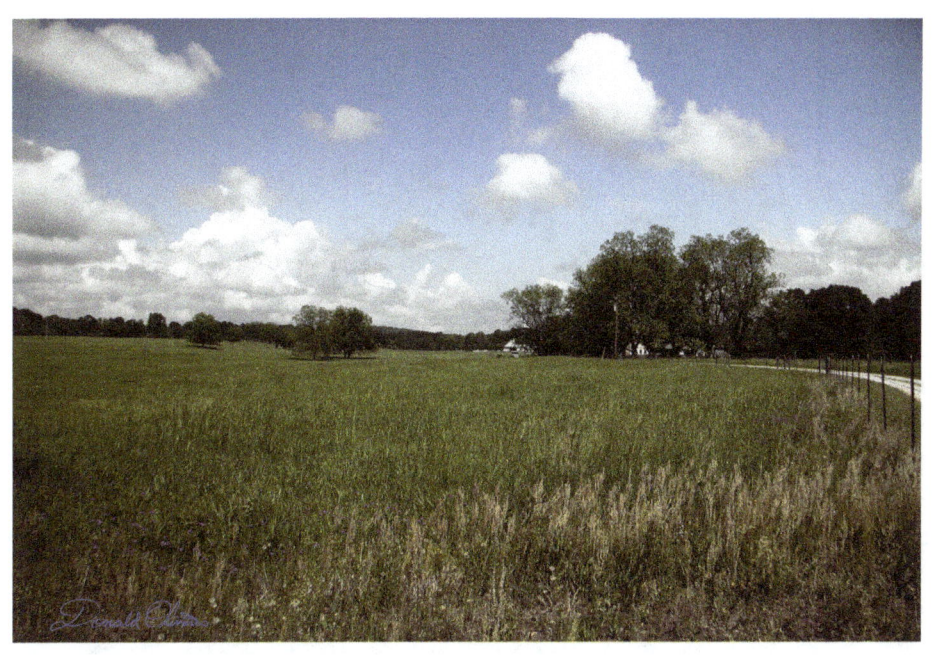

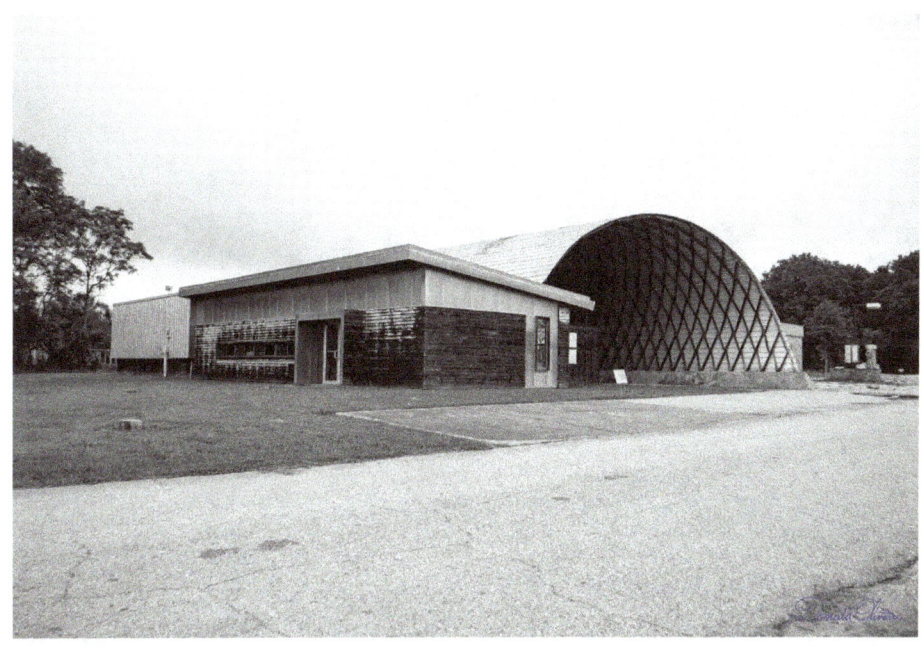

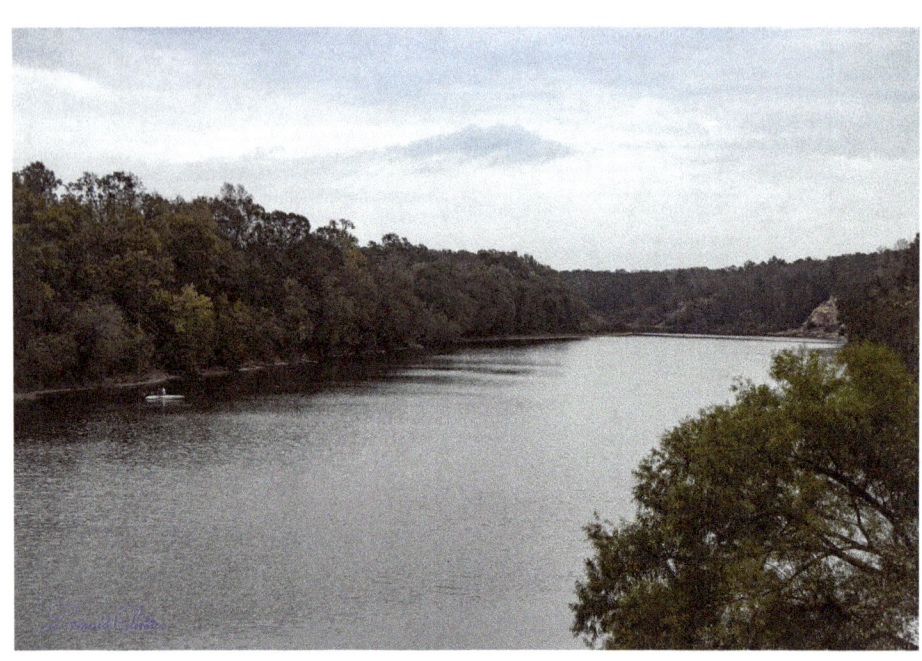

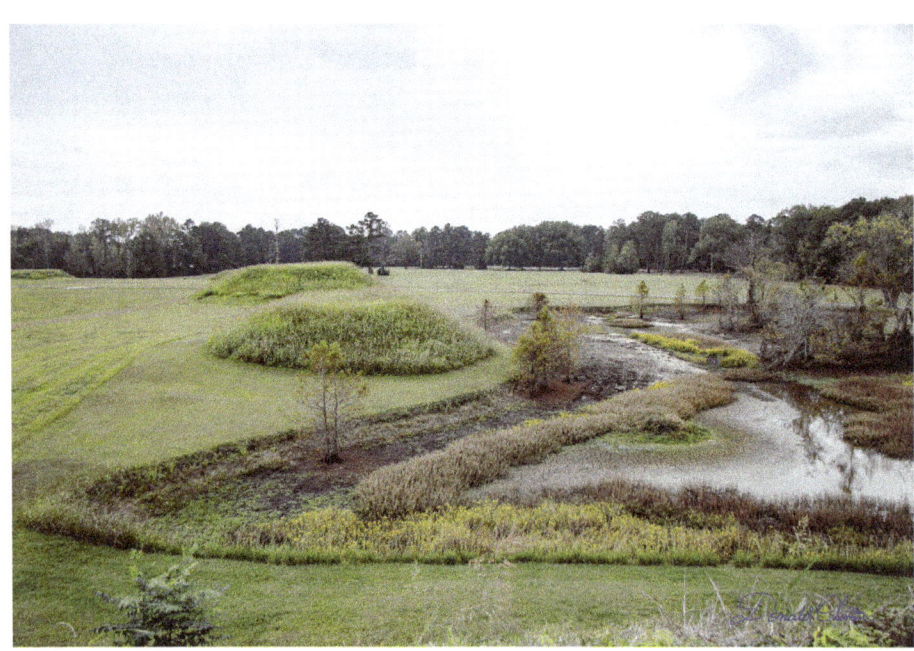

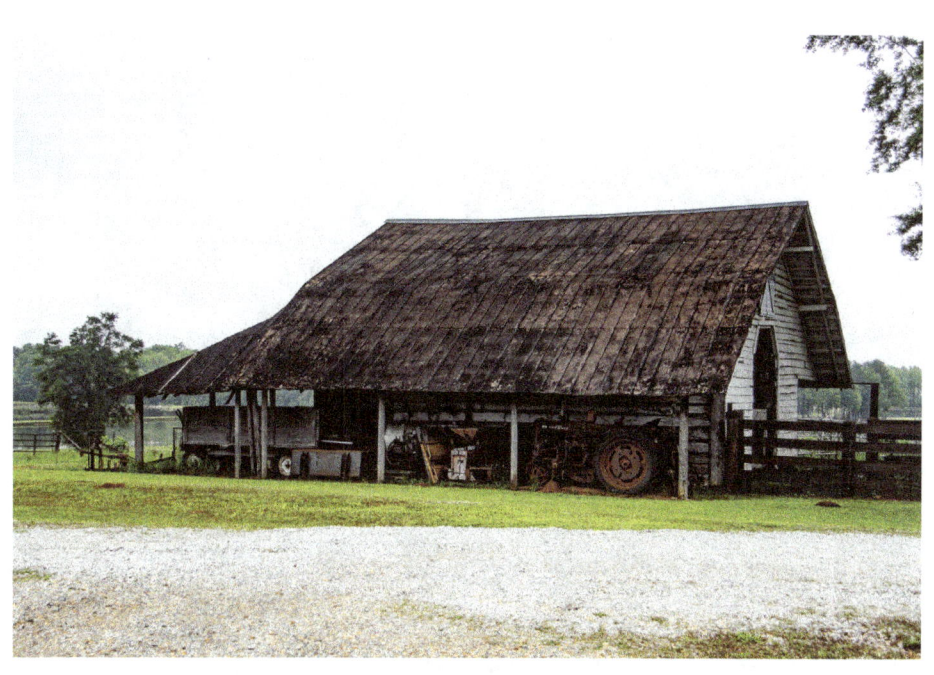

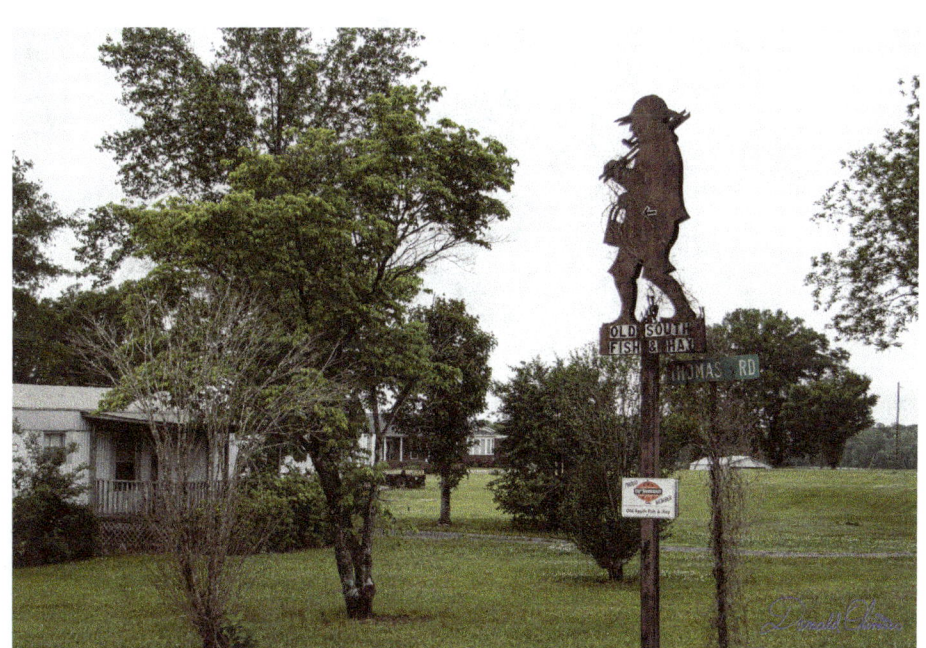

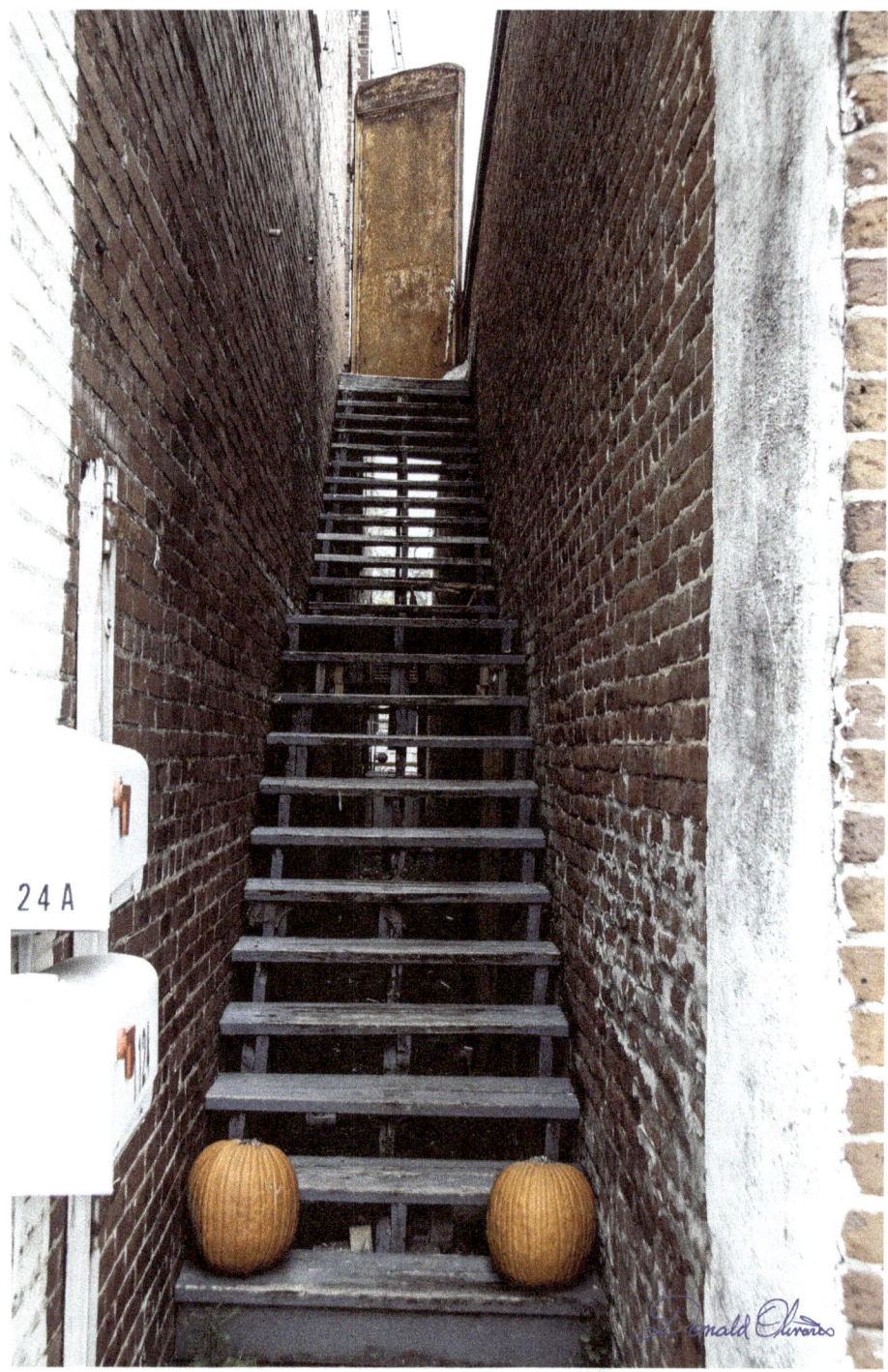

24 A

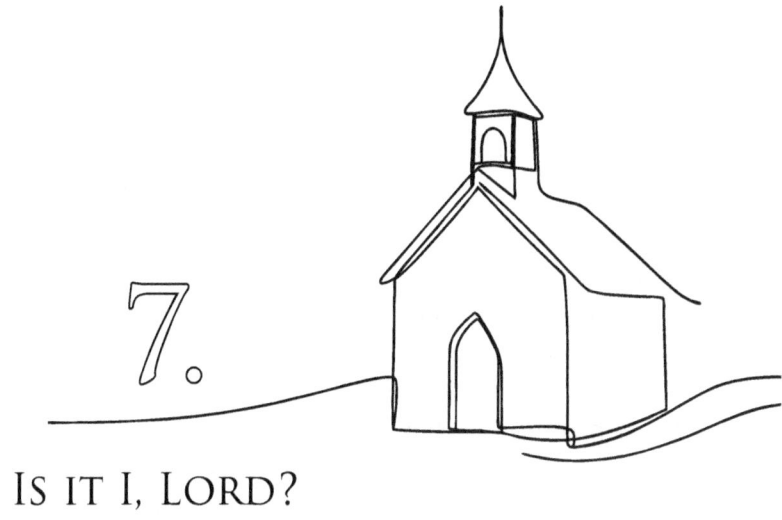

IS IT I, LORD?

Mark 14:17-19

And in the evening he cometh with the twelve. And as they sat and did eat, Jesus said, Verily I say unto you, One of you which eateth with me shall betray me. And they began to be sorrowful, and to say unto him one by one, Is it I? and another said, Is it I? (KJV)

As Jesus sat with the disciples at the Last Supper (the Lord's Supper as we know it) he had many things that he wanted to share with his disciples. There were many thoughts and feelings and plans - aware that physically he would not be alive much longer upon this earth. But one of the statements that Jesus shared with the disciples, as they gathered there in the upper room, was to them quite a shocking statement.

Jesus, as he looked over the group, was to say to them, "One of you will betray me." And almost immediately the replies of the disciples came, "Is it I, Lord?"

For our thinking this morning I would like for us to turn to this thought or this statement of the disciples and see what it has to say to us as we live in the latter quarter of the 20th century.

I

I think the first thing that it says to us is that it reveals that the disciples knew so little about themselves and, in all honesty, it is the same for us. We know so a little about ourselves. These men that Jesus is speaking to – one would betray him, the rest would either deny him by their voice or by the cover of night.

Let's remember that these men had given up home and family and job and all the old way of life that they had become accustomed to, to walk with him for three years. And when Jesus said, "One of you will betray me," they became consciously aware that they might not have the strength that they thought they had. That they might not quite understand the commitment that Jesus was calling them to and so there was a question in their minds, "Were they capable of betraying?" Or, we could add "of denying?" or "Forsaking him?"

And they all were. You know, Peter did not envision himself as a weak person. He envisioned himself as a very strong person. He could not imagine that somehow he would go and leave his Lord to suffer alone, for he was to remind Jesus, "Lord, if you must die, I will die with you."

But, also, the other disciples agreed to this. Peter did not know his weakness until he stood in the courtyard and there were those who began to question him. He found that he did not know himself.

I would suggest that we too, as God's people sometimes do not know ourselves. We think that as a disciple of Christ we would never betray or deny him. We would always be faithful to him. We would always be faithful to his church, his mission here on earth. And yet, as we see what happened to these the twelve men that walked with Jesus, that loved him, that trusted him with their lives, it seems if one could be capable of betraying and one denying and the rest fleeing, then surely it would call for us to begin to ask ourselves, "Is it I, Lord? Would I betray you? Would I deny you? Would I forsake you in the times of difficulty?"

Webster has his definition of betrayal: "one who helps the enemy." There comes the question in our hearts and minds as we come to communion, a time of looking in, of introspection, of seeing what kind of courage and commitment we have - would we help the enemy? Would we help the powers of sin and evil by not loving as Christ has called us to love? Would we help the powers of evil by not praying to be strengthened by God? Would we help the enemies of Christ by not caring or worshiping or serving?

Webster had yet another definition for the word betrayal; the word betrayal means to break the faith with, to no longer trust. And I suppose as we stop and look at this, this is something that we as Twentieth Century Christians have to wrestle with.

Do we trust Christ in the hard things of life? When Christ said, "Love your enemies, pray for those persecute you" there comes the searching of the soul. Have we experienced this kind of trust in Christ that we can follow him when he challenges us to do the hard things of life? When he challenges us to commit ourselves completely to him, placing our lives in his hands? Have we betrayed him by taking his name and going out into the world and living as we please, not letting the spirit of Christ guide us?

So, we need to hear the words of the disciples as they ask, "Is it I, Lord?" Have I betrayed you by not keeping the faith? By failing to follow where you would lead, have I failed you? Have I failed you because of selfishness and self-centeredness?

It reveals to us how much we need to examine our lives and our hearts in his presence. You know the lovely thing about the sanctuary and the worship service is the time when each and, in our own way, can come and look at our hearts and our minds and we can let the word of God speak to us and let him take away the those things which are not Christlike. And let him strengthen those things that are.

It is a great privilege to be part of a church where we come in the hour of worship and let his word speak to us in such a dramatic way. And we can come to know ourselves a little better.

II

The second thing that we see it revealing is, not only that the disciples knew so little about themselves, the statement reveals how little they knew about our Lord. You know the disciples were always getting confused about what was the mission and the ministry of Christ Jesus.

When they entered Jerusalem, the disciples were convinced that Jesus was going to allow them to crown him king. Some of the followers of Jesus were quite upset because Jesus refused on the first day – Palm Sunday –when he came riding into town. When he refused to accept the last step of saying, "All right I'm willing to be your king." Because, somehow they believed with all their hearts that Jesus came to establish an earthly ministry. They knew so little about his mission, his ministry.

There is a theory in the life of the church that the reason that Judas sold Jesus for thirty pieces of silver was that Judas believed with all his heart that Jesus would become king if simply he was forced in the issue. And if he was captured by the powers that be, that he would call down from heaven a legion of angels that would set him free. But even that theory points out how little the disciples knew of the nature and the mission of our Lord.

And so, as we come and look at ourselves, as we prepare our hearts to receive communion, we need to come and ask the question, "How much do we know about his mission? His ministry?" They thought it was an earthly kingdom he came to build. Sometimes, we in the life of the church, think that the kingdom of God is added to by blocks and bricks and stone as we erect a beautiful edifice for worshiping.

Sometimes we forget that the kingdom of God is within our midst. It is the transformation of the heart and the mind and the soul until we come to love what God loves and to despise that which is despicable in God's sight. All of us need to come every now and then (with no exceptions - all of us) and ask the question, "What is the nature in the ministry of our Lord?"

For if we forget what he's trying to do in the hearts and lives of people then we are sure to go in the wrong direction. The disciples were to say, "Is it I, Lord? Have I missed the mark? Have I gone to the wrong direction? Have I viewed your ministry wrongly?"

The third thing it reveals, this statement, it reveals how much, how deep Christ knows us. Jesus didn't say to the disciples gathered there in the upper room, "It's possible that one of you might betray me" but with a certainty he said, "One of you will betray me."

He said to Simon Peter - after Simon Peter had bragged about how brave he was – Jesus said, "After you've returned, strengthen the brethren." Consciously aware that Simon Peter would deny him and go his own way. You know the one thing in the Christian faith which is a comforting knowledge is that we can know that God loves and knows us. He knows our hearts and our minds. He knows when we go down the wrong path in our thoughts even if our actions have not yet followed.

And thank God he does because so often the gentleness of his love can pull us back to the right path before we make some tragic mistake. God's amazing knowledge of us is revealed as Jesus said to the disciples, "One of you will betray me." The disciples were aware that he knew. I hope that we are also consciously aware that God knows our minds, our thoughts, our dreams, our hopes, our aspirations.

But I think most important of all this statement that Jesus made to the disciples and their answer are not only reveals how little they knew about themselves and how little they knew about his mission and how much he understood their minds, but most important, it reveals how Jesus loved them.

For when Jesus was in agony, here in the upper room and now later in the garden, no words of bitterness cross his lips because of the disciples were betraying and forsaking him but rather we see the words of love, the words of healing, the words that tie back together the brokenness of the relationship. When Jesus said, "Father, forgive them for they know not what they do" to the ones that crucified him, how much more did he pray for the inner circle of the disciples. The twelve. The men that had walked with him in love and care. He ministers to them again.

In the words of "Is that I, Lord?" to Jesus breaking the meal to the disciples after they had been fishing on the Sea of Galilee all night, we find the culmination of the question, "Is it I, Lord?" Peter comes and has no words for our Lord. He denied him. The rest forsook him. Judas has betrayed him. What could they say?

And yet, Jesus with open arms and open heart welcomes them back. He didn't take away his mission from them but he encouraged them, "Feed my sheep." He reminded them that they still had a mission, a task. And it is what Jesus reminds us as we come and examine our hearts and minds and souls in his presence.

At times we all have sinned and fallen short of his glory. All of us have betrayed him by giving aid to the enemy. All of us have betrayed him by failing to keep faith. All of us have denied him by failing to put him first in our lives, at times.

But the lovely part of the story comes when he ties together the brokenness. Not our failure, but his love is always the triumph of the church. If our failure was the mark of the church, then the church would've never lasted this long. If our failure was the mark of our faith, then our faith would've not lasted this long. But the great thing in the Christian faith is his love. It is broader than our failure and deeper than our rebellion. His love is that which ties us back together that we might come again to receive his strength, to receive his guidance and to receive his cleansing.

That is what communion is all about.

Jesus comes to remind us that we take again his grace, his love. Not that we have used the other wisely, but forgetting the past, straining forward into the future we come to accept his love again and his forgiveness again that the brokenness of life might be made whole by his love.

CAST YOUR BURDENS
ON THE LORD

Psalms 55:22

Cast your cares on the Lord and he will sustain you; he will never let the righteous be shaken.

Matthew 11: 29-30

"Come to me, all you who are weary and burdened, and I will give you rest. Take my yoke upon you and learn from me, for I am gentle and humble in heart, and you will find rest for your souls. For my yoke is easy and my burden is light."

This morning as I come to share with you some of my thoughts on casting your burdens on the Lord, I come with a great sense of fear and trembling. Because I am consciously aware that this is one of the most difficult subjects that we have as Christians to deal with. Every one of us has problems and burdens that are very heavy for us to carry or bear. Sometimes we look at other people very wistfully and say, "I wish my life was like their life." But, when we become knowledgeable of the problems and the burdens and the heartaches that they bear, we become consciously aware that every pathway of life has its difficulty.

Every pathway of life has its burdens and its problems. And so, this morning we come to find if there is an aid, a strength, a sense of relief from the problems and the burdens that we bear. For therein we will find the secret of life.

First of all, I would share with you the words of the psalmist in the fifty-fifth psalm and the twenty second verse: "Cast thy burdens upon the Lord and he shall sustain thee." Now the psalmist was telling of the struggle of his own soul before this verse. Of how his problems had been many and how he had sought to escape. How he thought it would be best if, somehow, he could just pretend that he didn't have any problems - just leave them behind. But he said, "You know, I can't do that. I tried and it doesn't work." And as he struggled with all the ways of dealing with problems finally at last he came to the conclusion that the only way to deal with problems was to cast them upon the Lord, "And he shall sustain thee."

There are two things I would look to at this point. First of all, the burdens or the problems that we have, when we cast them upon the Lord, do not cease to exist. They are still ours. We still have to deal with them. And yet, now we have someone far wiser, far more loving, far stronger than we are that helps us to bear it. He didn't say, "Cast your burdens upon the Lord and they are gone." He said, "Cast your burdens upon the Lord and he shall sustain thee." Sometimes people get the wrong impression of how we solve the problem of burden.

It reminds me of a story that happened in the town that I grew up in. There was a man who went around getting credit from every store that he could in town until finally at last he owed about as many people as they would allow him to owe. And they were upset because they couldn't collect the money from him. And so, whenever they went to town all the merchants and the people that had loaned him money would begin to ask him for what he owed them. One night he, in an emotional furor quote, unquote, got saved. And the next morning he was walking down the streets of the town and the merchants stopped him and said, "Hey, how about paying me the bill that you owe me?" And he said, "Oh, haven't you heard? I got saved last night and I turned my debts over to the Lord."

Well, you know, that wasn't what the psalmist was talking about. He isn't saying, "Turn our debts or our burdens or our problems over to him." He says, "Cast them upon me and I shall sustain thee, strengthen thee, guide thee." God wants to know the problems and the heartaches and the hurts that we have. And we need to cast them upon him in such a fashion that he shares with us. Bu, more important that we allow him to share with us his sustaining love, his sustaining strength. They are still our burdens. They are still our problems. But now, God is helping us to understand and to see and to share with us his strength that we might have a way of solving those problems. Or, if not solving them, learning to live with them. Because there are some burdens, some problems that we do not find a simple solution to.

St. Paul had his struggle. The thorn in the flesh that plagued him was something that stayed with him as long as he lived. But he found God's strength sufficient for his need at that point.

The second thing that I would share with us as the psalmist is talking to us about casting our burdens upon the Lord, is that to cast burdens upon him we have to learn to trust God. That is not always easy to do. We cast burdens so seldom upon God. We keep them to ourselves. Maybe we can understand our dilemma a little bit better if we look at how we tend to cast away or throw away other things.

We throw away our opportunities sometimes too easily. Every now and then I see a young person throwing away their future in frivolous living. I see us casting away so many things that are near and dear to us but, sometimes we have the tendency to hold our burdens, our problems. We keep them close to us. We don't trust them to God or to anyone else.

Several years ago, when I was in another parish, on a Sunday night when I had finished preaching and I had gotten back to the parsonage the phone rang. On the other end of the line was a man who had been at church that night. He was one of the pillars of the church. He was always there on Sunday morning and Sunday night and he was very faithful in all of his activities in the life of the church. But, he was a burdened person. He was always worried. He was always bowed down by the things of the past.

So, when I heard his voice on the other end of the line I wondered if something had gone wrong that night and I called his name and I said, "Is something wrong?" And he said, "Yes, but it is me. Would you meet me at my office?" And I said, "When do you want me to meet you?" And he said, "Right Now!"

So, I got back in the car and I drove back to his office and we sat there in the confines of that little office a few moments and he began to tell me about how burdened he was. And he said, "Preacher, what can I do? What can I do?" And I looked at him and there was so much that was lovable about this man. I looked at him and I said, "You know, if you could only let God share this burden with you." And he said, "What is my burden? I find them in all directions But what is my real burden?"

And I said, "Guilt. Guilt about something you never did but that someone did and you took the responsibility and you have never put it down." For, he was in the Second World War and he had a father who was a very powerful man. And his daddy found him a place where he didn't have to go and serve his country when it was dangerous. He was on the home front doing the little things while his buddies were out being shot up in Italy and in France and in the South Pacific.

Tears began to stream down his cheeks and he said, "Preacher, you are right. All these years I've been carrying this burden of feeling guilty about what someone else did that I couldn't understand. And every time I saw one of my buddies come home with a limp or every time I saw one of my buddies come home with an arm missing, I felt so guilty that I felt that I didn't have a right to live!"

And I said to him, "That burden is not yours alone. Let God share it with you. Let his love undergird you and sustain you until the forgiveness cleanses you of all the problems that you feel."

You know, we throw away a lot of things but sometimes we won't throw away the thing that we ought to. We won't cast our burden on the Lord and let him share it with us until we understand it.

The third thing that I would share with us is what Jesus said. Not what the psalmist said. I think two of the loveliest verses in the New Testament are found in the Gospel of Matthew in the last two verses of the eleventh chapter when Jesus looked at the crowd and said, "Come unto me all ye that labor and are heavy laden."

For he was consciously aware that the reason that the people were there that heard him gladly out there in the semi-desert aridness of his land was because their burdens were heavy. And they had found no relief from their burdens, their heartaches, their problems, their pains. And Jesus said, "Come to me that you might find some relief. Trust in me."

I think of the story of the rich young ruler. He came to Jesus with burdens, with problems, but he didn't learn to trust. And you know what happened. He went away the same way he came. He went away sorrowfully, with a broken heart, with a broken spirit. Feeling the emptiness of life because he couldn't trust his life to Jesus.

On the other hand, I think of someone like the tax collector, Matthew. Burdened down, consciously aware that somehow all the money he had made no difference in the joys of life he was seeking because he couldn't buy them. But Jesus said, "Follow me."

The first Gospel that we have written in the New Testament is the Gospel that bears his stamp, his image. Matthew saw Jesus as one who gave the perfect law that opened to hiom the doorway of life. But Matthew had to trust him. Matthew had to closeup his little shop. Tie up his little bags and turn to his partner and say, "From henceforth you are the man that collects the taxes. I follow Jesus."

And I will say to us this morning that I don't know what your burdens are but until we learn to trust our Lord Jesus Christ with our lives, our burdens will never go away or never be solved. And they will not necessarily go away immediately when our trust begins. We will not necessarily find a solution right then, but we will find a strength, a sustaining power. One who cares also gives us a yoke that we can bear.

So, I would challenge us this morning to hear the words of our Lord, "Follow me." You know, learning to trust is like learning to swim. You have to give yourself up to the water before you can swim. If you get rigid you sink like a rock. I know, because I am non-swimmer. I don't trust the water very well. I have a real struggle with this point. But on a few occasions when I can float, I learned that I had to relax.

Trusting our Lord Jesus is this way. We have to put our lives in his hands. There comes the question, "Why should we trust God? Why should we trust our Lord Jesus Christ to bear our burdens and care for us?"

I would say first of all because he is trustworthy. He is trustworthy. Our heavenly Father who made us and called us into being is one who made this great universe that we are part of. Not just this universe but this cosmos. My, what a creation this is! If we were to go from one side of this cosmos to the other at the speed of light, 186,000 miles a second (I can't even imagine moving that fast), it would take us two hundred years to cross from one side to the other side of just this cosmos that God has made in such beautiful, perfect order. Every body, every planet pulls against the other in a perfect rhythm. God is trustworthy, for he has made this universe in such a marvelous and wonderful fashion. More than that, he has made us. He has made us in such a marvelous and wonderful fashion and called us to be his children. He loves us! He cares about us. He is trustworthy.

You know, we live in a world where trust sometimes is a very precious commodity. Not long ago I was in a store and they finger-printed me when they took my check. They said that it was for my safety. I wasn't really worried about that. I was worried about whether they were going to take my check or not. I have had them photograph me. You can go into a place and they will take your picture with your check so that they can identify you. And you ask them about the third time and they get to know you and they say, "But, we get so many bad checks that we can't trust people."

One of the great things in life as a Christian is that we can trust God. For God loves and cares for us. God sustains us. God enables us to live the fullness of life because he is there. Whenever we go to him he is there. Sometimes we can't get through to him because of our problems but he is always reaching out with a loving hand, caring for us.

And that is the second reason we can trust God because he loves us. He loves us more than we can really understand. I can understand the fact that he has made us and that he has called us to be his own. But, it stretches my mind to come to understand the fact that he loves us so much that he sent his son. And that he was willing that his son die that we might know the magnitude of his love. We can trust him because he loves us.

We can also trust him because he alone can handle many of the burdens of life that we have. There are problems that I have and that you have that we can't solve. We can't solve them by ourselves. It is the height of arrogance sometimes when we believe that we can solve all of our problems by ourselves because we can't.

What do we do in the hour of sorrow? In the moments of loss? It is not our strength. It is God's strength that sustains us. What do we do when we have done everything we can in our power to understand a person or a situation and we find that we always draw a blank. We turn to God. For God is the sustaining power, the sustaining strength. He can handle the problems that we can't handle.

The thing that I love about the psalmist in the fifty fifth psalm was because he became aware that the problems that he had - he couldn't solve. He needed some help.

I have a very dear friend who is a psychiatrist. When he was in Medical School there was a problem, that he had, as he was working it on his chemistry test. He couldn't solve it his way. And the professor told him there was another way. And as the professor told him there was another way this doctor said, "No, I've got to do it my way." And the professor said, "Well, I'm sorry but it will never be solved your way." And the doctor said, "But, I think I can solve it my way."

When the finals came that problem was the last problem. When everybody else finished and turned-in their papers, this man was still there working on that problem. And the professor came in and said, "Are you convinced now?"

I think sometimes God must look at us and he hears us say, "I can solve my problem by myself." And he loves us and he pities us and he says, 'Oh, I wish you could learn."

There are some problems that you can't ever solve by yourself. Only with the strength of his love and his care and the guidance of his wisdom can we ever solve some problems. He is trustworthy because he can solve the problems or lead us into an understanding of his greatness that is strength enough for our walking the Road of Life.

And lastly, and most important, we can trust him because he alone is the one that gives us newness of life. He alone is the one who gives to us newness of life. For there is a spiritual source of strength that our hearts and minds must know to know the abundant life. Our Lord is trustworthy because he comes to supply our hearts and minds with the spiritual needs that we have.

As surely as we go to the table and eat a well-prepared meal that our bodies might be sustained physically, so we come to God that his spirit might sustain us spiritually and renew our heart and minds and lives. He is trustworthy because he loves us, because he guides us, because he is true, because he is able.

I don't know what you are going to do with your burdens or problems, but I know how God can help us if we will share them with him. For he can be our source of strength and our source our source of comfort and our guiding hand if we trust our lives to his care.

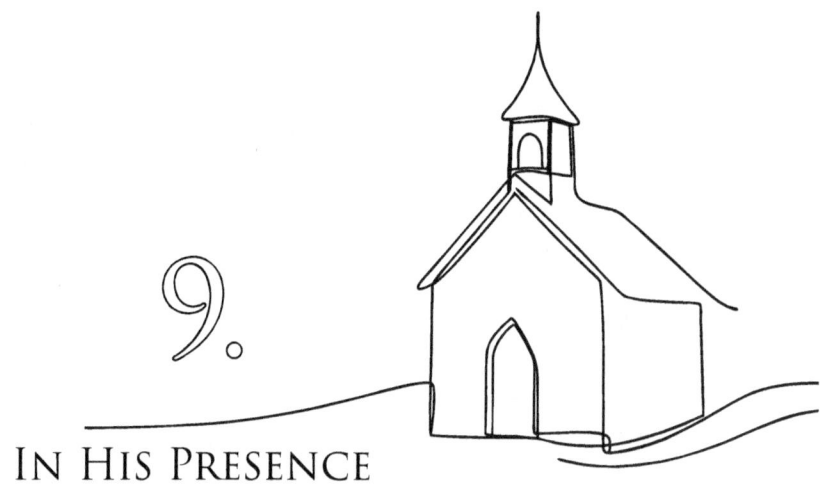

9.

In His Presence

John 21:1-17

Afterward Jesus appeared again to his disciples, by the Sea of Galilee. It happened this way: Simon Peter, Thomas (also known as Didymus), Nathanael from Cana in Galilee, the sons of Zebedee, and two other disciples were together. "I'm going out to fish," Simon Peter told them, and they said, "We'll go with you." So they went out and got into the boat, but that night they caught nothing. Early in the morning, Jesus stood on the shore, but the disciples did not realize that it was Jesus. He called out to them, "Friends, haven't you any fish?" "No," they answered. He said, "Throw your net on the right side of the boat and you will find some." When they did, they were unable to haul the net in because of the large number of fish. Then the disciple whom Jesus loved said to Peter, "It is the Lord!" As soon as Simon Peter heard him say, "It is the Lord," he wrapped his outer garment around him (for he had taken it off) and jumped into the water. The other disciples followed in the boat, towing the net full of fish, for they were not far from shore, about a hundred yards. When they landed, they saw a fire of

burning coals there with fish on it, and some bread.
Jesus said to them, "Bring some of the fish you have
just caught." So Simon Peter climbed back into the
boat and dragged the net ashore. It was full of large
fish, 153, but even with so many the net was not torn.
Jesus said to them, "Come and have breakfast." None
of the disciples dared ask him, "Who are you?" They
knew it was the Lord. Jesus came, took the bread and
gave it to them, and did the same with the fish. This
was now the third time Jesus appeared to his disciples
after he was raised from the dead. When they had fin-
ished eating, Jesus said to Simon Peter, "Simon son of
John, do you love me more than these?" "Yes, Lord,"
he said, "you know that I love you." Jesus said, "Feed
my lambs." Again Jesus said, "Simon son of John, do
you love me?" He answered, "Yes, Lord, you know
that I love you." Jesus said, "Take care of my sheep."
The third time he said to him, "Simon son of John,
do you love me?" Peter was hurt because Jesus asked
him the third time, "Do you love me?" He said, "Lord,
you know all things; you know that I love you." Jesus
said, "Feed my sheep."

Something strange and wonderful happens to those that walk
with Jesus. Those that commit their lives to the power of his love
and his wisdom. This morning, I would like for us to spend a
little time thinking together about what happened to Simon Peter
because he chose to live his life in the presence of the Master. But,
also I would like for us to spend some time asking the question of
ourselves, "What are the things that need to happen in our lives as
we continue to try to walk with him, too."

First of all, in his presence we come to see, to face and to know our sinful condition. There is a lovely story in the Gospel of Luke in the fifth chapter that has some amazing similarities to the story in the twenty first chapter of the Gospel of John. The story is different in many ways and yet, those similarities are the fact that Peter is fishing. And here he catches a great number of fish because Jesus challenges him to put down the net on the other side of the boat.

In the gospel of Luke it's the beginning of the ministry of our Lord and Peter does not know our Lord very well at that time. And so, when Jesus comes to preach to the crowd that had gathered on the Sea of Galilee that morning, he realized that there were more people there than could see him or hear what he was saying unless he got into the boat and moved out from the shore a little piece.

And when he got into the boat, and got Peter to move the boat out a little piece, then he delivered his message and after he finished his message then he challenged Peter to let down the net for the catch. The result was that they caught more fish they could imagine. Simon Peters' first reaction was not a reaction of amazement at the number of fish that he caught or the fact that Jesus knew the fish were there. The reaction was a facing of his own sinfulness and the purity of Christ. He cried out, "Depart from me! I am a sinful man."

When he came face-to-face with Jesus. When he lived for a few moments in his presence. When he heard him share the word of God in that morning message that he gave, it must've touched the heart of Peter in such a fashion that he could honestly see the things that he had done and the things that he wasn't doing and the things that his selfish heart made him want to do that were not Christlike. And all of a sudden when this miracle took place he said, "Lord, depart from me, for I'm a sinner."

I think that one of the most amazing things that happens to us as we come to live in the presence of our Lord is that we come to an awareness of our sins. Dr. Samuel Shoemaker, one of the great evangelical spirits of the Episcopal Church in his book *How to Become a Christian* has these words to say: "Until a man or woman has learned to admit to himself or herself their own sins; [until then] Christianity has not yet begun."

I found it amazing as I was reading this particular book of his that he chose the next to the last chapter to make the statement. For before this he was endeavoring to help us to see the love and the magnitude and the wisdom of God. But then points out that if we live in his presence, if we allow ourselves to feel his spirit, there comes a time in our lives when we have to face our own sins, our own failures, our own shortcomings.

E. Stanley Jones was to say, "The greatest mission field today is the Church." Consciously aware that sometimes we tend to live our lives not in the presence of the Master but we simply let our Christian faith become a routine thing. We come and we study and we worship and then we go away the same person. And that is tragic but if we dare to live in his presence, we become aware of the things in my life and in your life that need changing.

And is not a once and always done thing that we can do it and forget it. For from the beginning of Jesus' ministry, as he touched the life of Simon Peter, until here we see him at the close of his earthly ministry - even after the resurrection - Simon Peter is having to face his sins.

You know, as we read the story in the Gospel of John of Simon Peter jumping overboard and rushing to meet the Master there on the shore of the Sea of Galilee, you notice there were no words exchange between Peter and our Lord when he got there. And I imagine that when he got there he became very much aware of his denial of Jesus. Of how, as he had stood in the courtyard of Annas and Caiaphas while Jesus was on trial and there were those who begin to point their accusing finger at Simon Peter and say to him, "You are one of them."

Simon Peter begins to curse and begins to deny in all kinds of fashions that he never knew Jesus. And you recall as Jesus looked at Peter and the cock was crowing, Peter begins to weep. Because the one thing that happened to Simon Peter was that as he lived in the presence of our Lord, he became aware of his sins and his sinful condition.

Every now and then I read some of the stories of some of the greatest saints that have ever lived and the one thing that always amazes me is that the closer they get to God the more they are aware of their sins. And this will happen to us if we dare to live in his presence. We come to experience his truth and his love and his wisdom as we become aware that our sins are not selfish little misdeeds of life. Their sins against love.

"For God so loved the world." For God so loved us. And when we say no to God and yes to self, we are not just breaking God's laws in some thrill of our own thought, but we are breaking his heart. We are choosing to go our way and not his way. And no greater love can man ever know than the love of God that has reached out to touch us and transform us.

And so, the first thing that happens to us as we live in the presence of Jesus is that we become aware of our sins and that our sins are sins against love. For God loves us. Each of us.

Then the second thing that happens to us as we live in his presence is that we come to experience the possibility of conversion. We come to experience the power of his presence. The difference between the first story I told you in the Gospel of Luke and the last story that we read where Simon Peter is faced with his sinfulness is the difference in Simon Peter and what he sees that God's power can do.

In the first time when he saw his sins he said, "Jesus, leave me alone. I can't be any better. I'm a bad fellow. I have a foul mouth. I do un-Christian things. Depart from me."

But, in the second one as he comes face-to-face with his sins he comes again to something else. The power of God's love to change, to transform, to cause him to be born anew. You notice when Jesus speaks to him the next time he doesn't say, "Depart from me," but he listens. And I can imagine we can begin to see Simon Peter dream. The dream of the day when he can be all that Jesus ever believed he could be and all that he prayed for him to be.

If we live in his presence long enough, we don't let our sins run us away from him. We let the power of his love transform us. Yes, we are going to sin and we're going to fall short but we know when we stand in his presence that his power can make a difference in our lives. We don't have to live in the same old way we used to live. We don't have to think the same way or feel the same way or act the same way. We don't have to be selfish anymore and self-centered.

Simon Peter learned that in his presence we can become Christ centered. And so, if we live in his presence, not only do we come to know our sins but we come to know the power of the gospel. The power of the good news can change and transform and remake us.

Thirdly, in his presence, not only do we come to face our sins and to experience his power, but in his presence we come to find courage to be his person. Simon Peter had not totally found the courage of being a man for the Master as he was in the courtyard while Jesus was on trial. But turn a little further in the Bible and you'll find one of the most amazing stories in the book of Acts. Jesus has been crucified but now he has been raised. The resurrection is a reality. And the disciples have experienced the power of God's presence in a fresh and a new way in their lives.

They begin to preach that Jesus is God's son, the Messiah. The Jews begin to get upset about this and then begin to try to find ways of discrediting their witness. Finally, at last when they could find no way to seal the mouth and the message of Peter, they put him in prison. They brought him into the Sanhedrin and then began to talk to he and John. And realizing that unless they took some extreme action these men were going out and preach again - they beat them.

When they finish beating them Simon Peter went out rejoicing because he had been counted worthy of suffering for the Master. There's something electrifying about this, for there was a man who was a coward who has become a man who is filled with courage. Here a man, who was afraid to admit that even knew Jesus, was now testifying to those who had the power to destroy him that Jesus Christ was Lord.

He found a new courage. Courage came because he lived in the presence of God. It didn't come because he joined a church, because he worshiped every now and then or because he had his doctrines right in his mind. It happened because he was open to God. And he lived his life in the presence of the One who loved and cared for him. And the One who loves and cares for us.

In our strength we find ourselves failing. By our own courage we find ourselves cowards. But, if we live in the presence of Christ not only do we come to see our sinful condition, and the power of God's love to transform us, but we find the courage to be his witness in this world, this day.

And then fourthly, in his presence we come to hear his call and understand his mission. We can't hear the call of our Lord or understand what he wants us to do until we live in his presence for a while. Simon Peter had been walking with him for three years and he had never quite got a clear vision of what Jesus wanted him to do. But, we see now at the closing story of the Gospel of John, Jesus is challenging him to serve his fellow man. He said, "Feed my lambs" and "Feed my sheep."

He was challenging him to go out in love and care and minister to those around him. And I hear our Lord challenging us. We are not going to hear the clear challenge or get a clear picture of his mission until we live in his presence. Until we are willing to face our sinful condition that can be changed only by his forgiveness and experience his power that can come to us only when we are willing to yield our lives to his control.

Conversion does not happen by an outward situation but by an inward change. The willingness to live life in his presence. To let his truth convict us of our sins so that his forgiveness and his love can cleanse and transform us.

May we in the coming days live in his presence in such a special way that the world can see Christ in us and hear his challenge through our message. We come at the communion service to meet Christ in a special way. May our hearts be open and receptive to the gift of grace that he would share with us as we come to partake of the Lord's Supper.

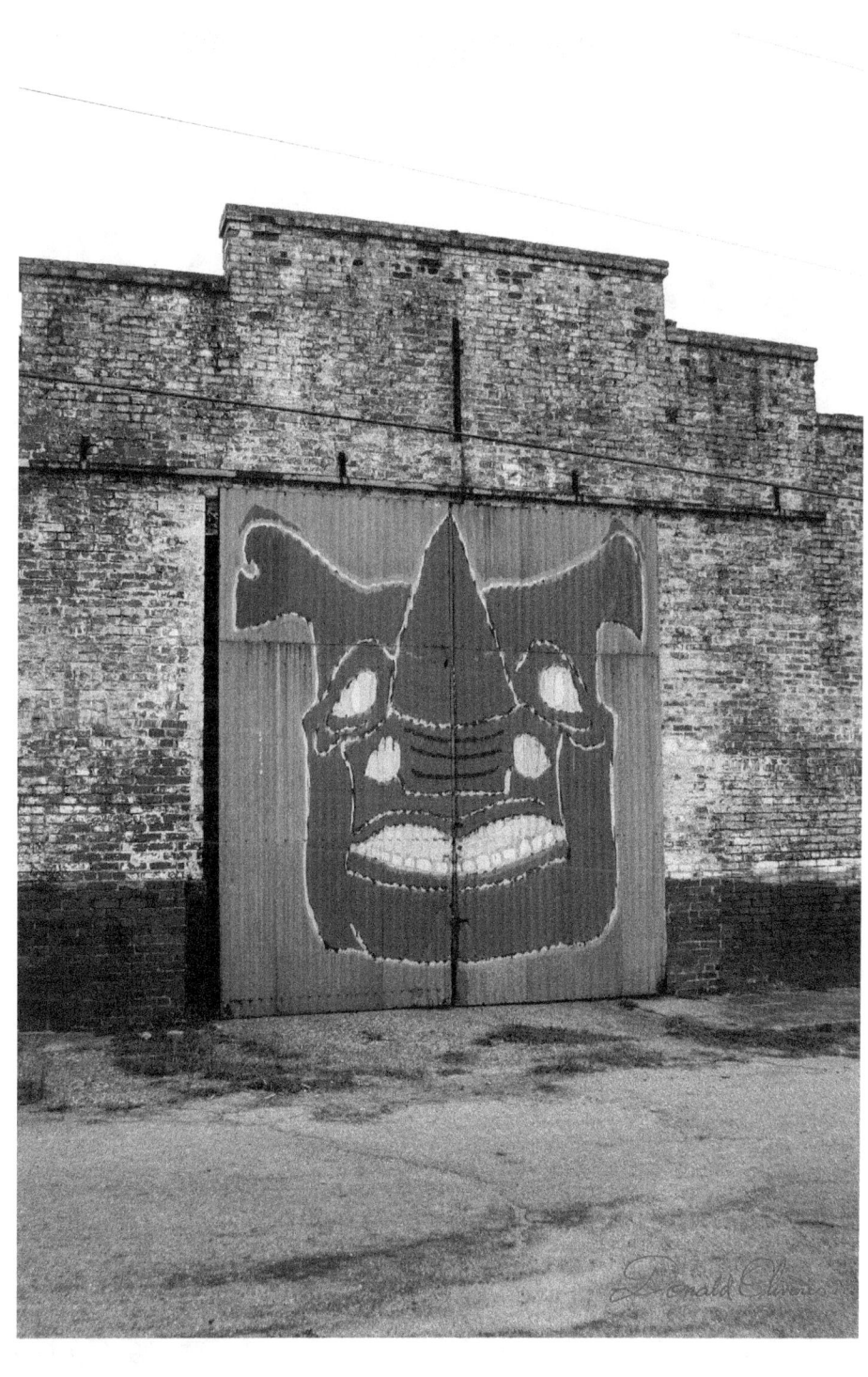

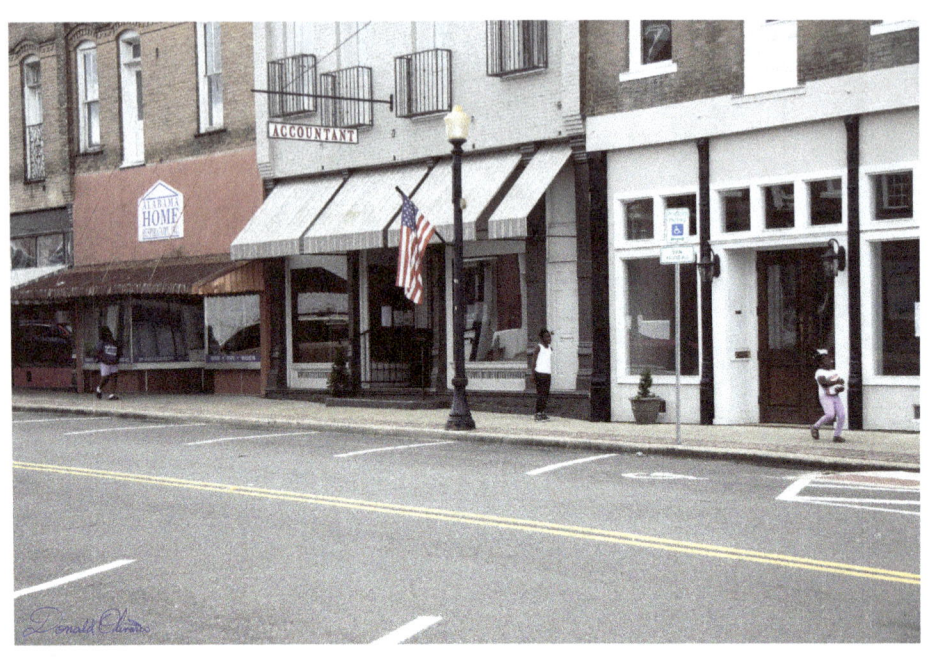

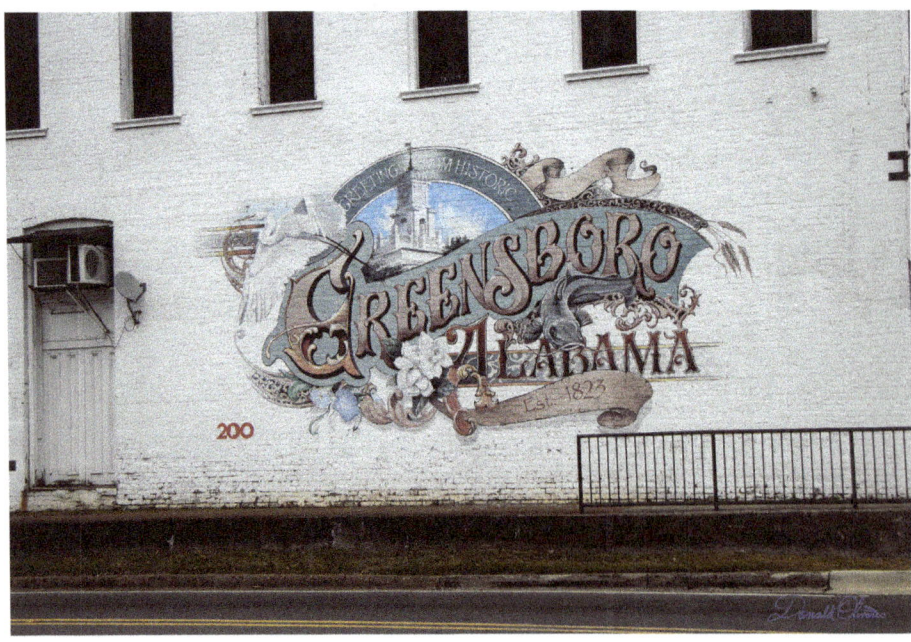

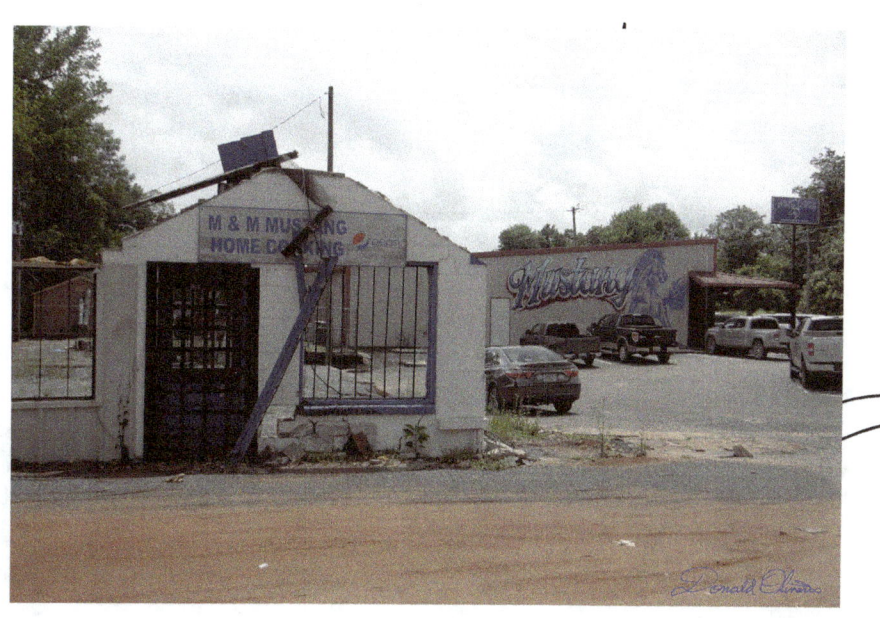

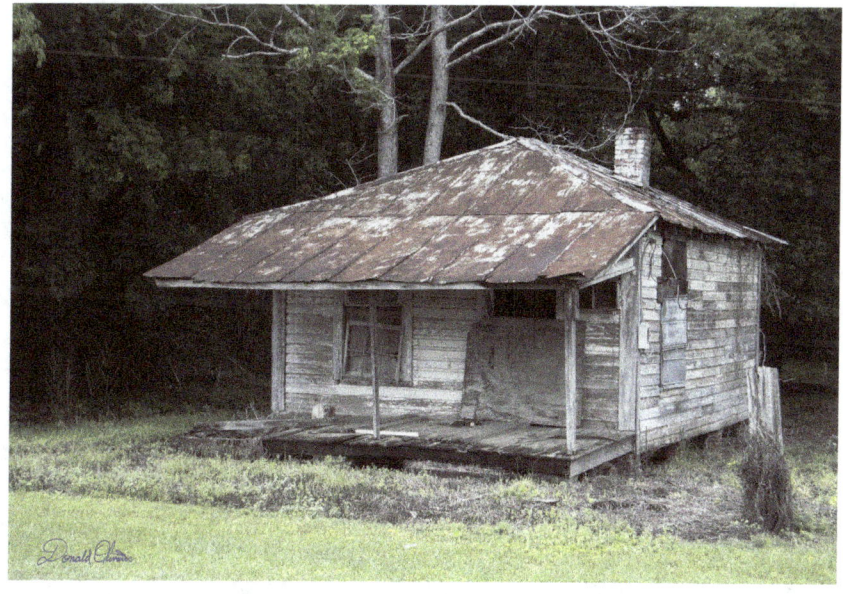

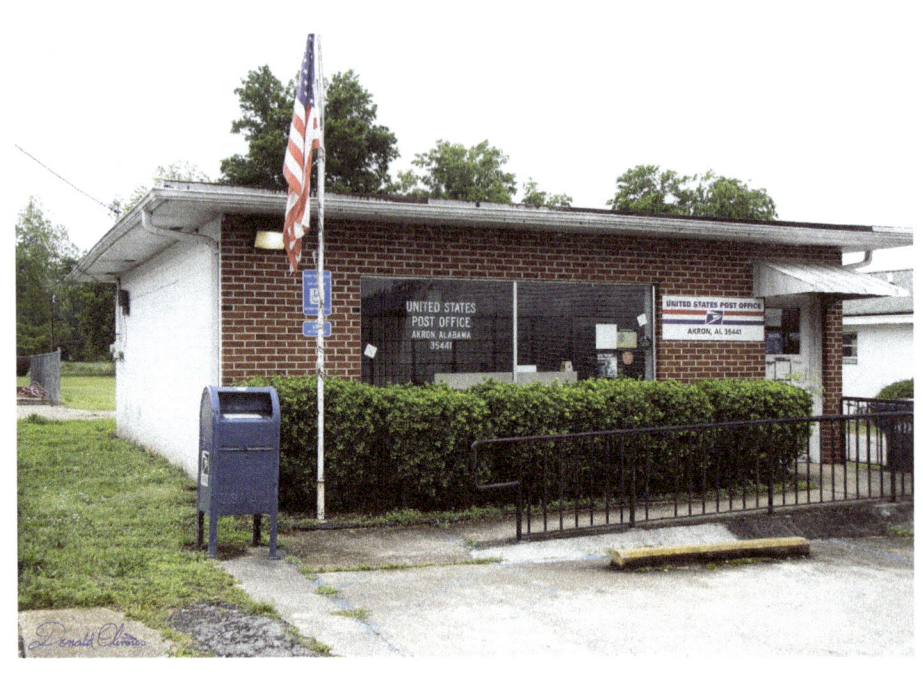

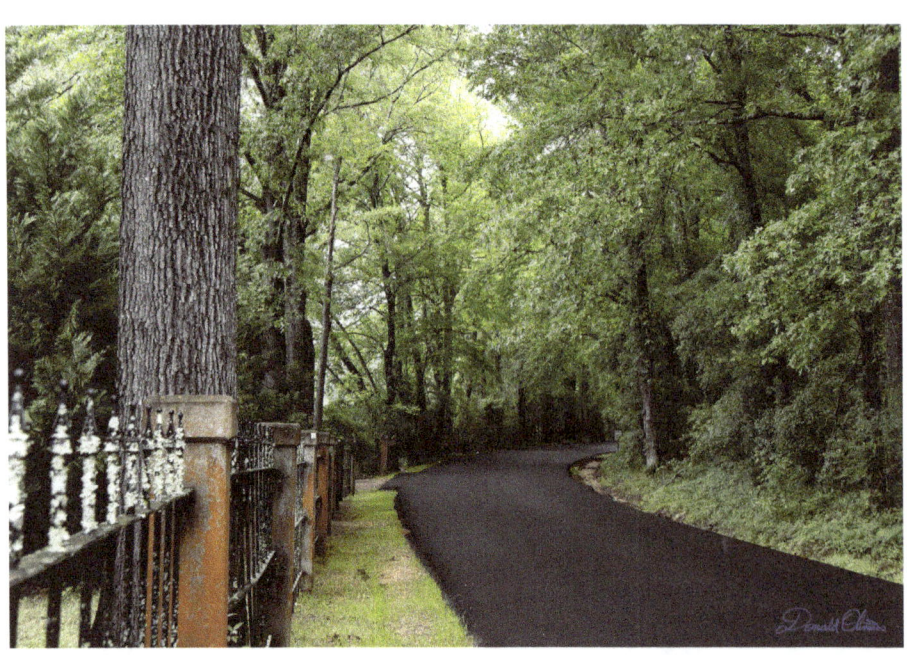

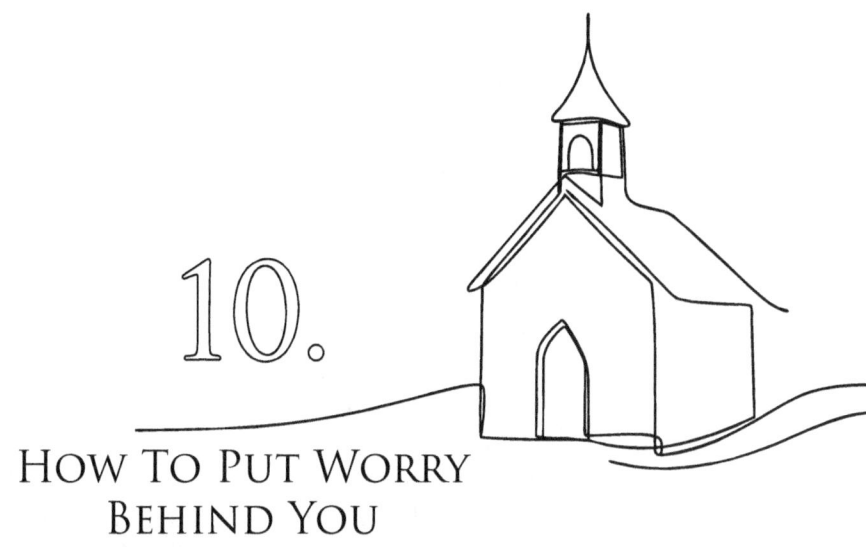

10.

How To Put Worry Behind You

Matthew 6:25-34

"Therefore, I tell you, do not worry about your life, what you will eat or drink; or about your body, what you will wear. Is not life more than food, and the body more than clothes? Look at the birds of the air; they do not sow or reap or store away in barns, and yet your heavenly Father feeds them. Are you not much more valuable than they? Can any one of you by worrying add a single hour to your life? "And why do you worry about clothes? See how the flowers of the field grow. They do not labor or spin. Yet I tell you that not even Solomon in all his splendor was dressed like one of these. If that is how God clothes the grass of the field, which is here today and tomorrow is thrown into the fire, will he not much more clothe you—you of little faith? So do not worry, saying, 'What shall we eat?' or 'What shall we drink?' or 'What shall we wear?' For the pagans run after all these things, and your heavenly Father knows that you need them. But seek first his kingdom and his righteousness, and all these things will be given to you as well. Therefore, do not worry about tomorrow, for tomorrow will worry about itself. Each day has enough trouble of its own."

I have a friend that lives in another town who calls quite often to tell me his troubles and his worries. In fact, the other morning he woke me up, calling to ask me if he could call me that night. I'm not kidding. Because he thought he might be worried and upset.

You know I don't think God meant for us to live life this way. And yet, worry and anxiety have been a part of human existence for a long, long time. In fact, even Jesus had to deal with it with people in his day. And so, he thought it was so important that he took time out on the Sermon on the Mount to deal with worry.

For a few moments this morning I would like for us to think about some of the things that he has said and some of the things that we find in the Gospel that give us some handles. So that we can deal with worry and put it behind us. And then get on with the task of living.

First of all, I hear Jesus saying that we should believe in God. Center our faith. Center our belief in God. We're creatures that believe in something. We all believe in something. And I would suggest that it makes a great deal of common sense to begin with to believe in something that will help us. Something that will make us better people.

I know and you know people who believe in worrying. They believe in looking for the bad things. They believe in looking for the disaster that is going to happen each day. And if the sun is shining, they are sure that they'll get blistered, and they will be too hot. If it's raining, it's going to be too much rain and it's going to be bad. And whatever the condition of life outside is there's always a way to make it worse than it is and they work on it.

Also, I know people who worry about other people. They worry about the bad in other people. They look for the bad. And you know, if you look for the bad long enough you usually find it, for all of us have flaws. All of us do things that are displeasing to someone else.

You know, those folks in the day of Jesus went around picking at Jesus. They didn't like it if he sat down and ate a meal with people that he wasn't supposed to (they thought). They didn't like it if he walked too far on the Sabbath day or healed somebody at the wrong time. They were always looking for the bad. They never could see the good. They didn't believe in God. They believed in trouble. They believed in evil. They believed in worry.

I know people today who called themselves Christians who believe more in the devil than they do in God. Because they are always giving the devil credit for everything. And they are giving the world back to him. And they're giving everybody they can find to him. But I don't believe that God meant for us to live life this way. Jesus reminds us that we are to believe in God. To believe in God because he is trustworthy. We can trust him with our lives.

I not only believe in God as one who is trustworthy, but I believe in the goodness of God. That he is working daily for our well-being. Long before man ever inhabited this planet, God was in the process of providing this kind of freeing atmosphere. That we might enjoy the richness and the fullness of life.

And, oh how we need to come to believe in the goodness of life that comes from God. Or the goodness of God. That he is trying to avail to us the best that's there.

Not only do we need to believe in the goodness of God but to believe in his love. To believe that he cares what happens to us. Jesus said, "Why should you go around worrying all the time? God already loves and cares for you and tries to minister to you." If simply we put our faith in him, then we can put down our worries, our anxieties, the things that cause life to become negative for us.

As I was thinking about learning to put down worrying, I begin to think about another friend I have. One who spends so much time worrying that if you took away his ability to worry he'd be unemployed. And you know, sometimes we might be the same way.

If magically our ability to worry were taken away, I wonder how many more hours of the day we would have. For we have a way of worrying ourselves to death. Worrying ourselves until life is spent. Jesus said we need to begin first of all with belief in God.

Secondly, we need to begin with the belief that life as a good gift from God. We need to look for the beautiful.

You know we have a hymn that reminds us that we need to spend our time looking for the beautiful. It doesn't take us long if we open our eyes to begin with to see the beauty. The beauty in God's creation. The beauty in His wisdom. The beauty in His love. The beauty in His people. We need not only to look for the beautiful, but we need to look for kindness.

Now one of the strange things in life is that we have a way, if we look for it we'll find kindness in the strangest places. The most unexpected places. But, there are so many good people. There are so many gentle and tenderhearted and loving and Christlike people in our world. And we miss so many of them if we don't begin by looking for kindness.

You know, so often people cover up their gentle and tender heart with a rough exterior and we miss them. We miss what they are really like unless we are willing to work at it. Unless we are really willing to look at the goodness of life and see the kindness of people.

Then we need not only to look for the beautiful and look for kindness, but we need to look for the blessings of God that he gives to us. The other day as I was thinking about the blessings that God gives us I begin to think one of the most beautiful solo hymns that used to be sung a great deal in the church: *The Love of God*. And in this hymn it tells us that if the sky was made of parchment and the ocean was filled with ink and if every man was a scribe by trade, to tell the love of God would drain the ocean dry. And the sky could not contain the whole if the scroll was stretched from sky to sky. Because that is how many blessings God has given us.

Oh, we're so tempted to zero in on the things that are wrong that sometimes we, as God's people need to stop and look back a little bit and ask the question, "What's right?" And when we begin the process we begin to see that God's blessings are always there. God loves us and cares for us.

And then thirdly, I would say that if we are going to put worry behind us, we not only have to trust God and see the goodness of life, but we have to live life with the undivided heart.

I suppose if there is anything that causes church members and Christians more anxiety than anything else it has to be the divided heart. To know the good and somehow in our selfishness want the wrong thing for ourselves. Wanting to somehow to serve God with one hand and self with the other.

This always creates worry and anxiety and tension. It is so easy for us to zero our thoughts on the things that we have and the things that we want instead of the God that provides them all. But when we live with a divided mind and a divided heart, worry and anxiety always becomes a part of our lives. God would not have us live with a divided heart. Jesus was very pointed at this point. He said, "You cannot serve two masters." You cannot serve selfish and self-centered thoughts and needs and plans and dreams and leave God out and be happy. And you can't serve yourself half the time and God half the time and be happy. There must be a getting together of your mind that you might serve God, with an undivided heart and an undivided mind.

Worry. Worry about what we eat or what we wear or where life is going to lead us reminds us that we have taken our eyes off of God for a little while and we've placed them on ourselves.

When we start the process of living a divided life, tension comes in. Anxiety becomes a way of life. Worry becomes the standard of the day. If we are going to put trouble behind us, if we are going to put worry behind us, we need to live with a unified mind - a mind which is centered on God.

Fourthly, if we are to put worrying behind us, not only do we need to believe in God and the goodness of life and the unity of our mind in our hearts, but we need also to make each day count. When Jesus was talking to the people at the Sermon on the Mount, he was to remind them that we can't live in yesterday and we can't live in tomorrow. We can't let yesterday's problems drag us down and we can't do anything about tomorrow yet.

Each day has troubles enough of its own. He called for his people in that day to live each day at a time. And he would call for us to do the same. To not allow the failures of the past to keep us from enjoying today. To not allow the fears of tomorrow to keep us from gleaning the richness of life from each hour of the day.

If we want to put worry behind us we have to make each day count. Live it to its fullest. Every now and then I see someone who says to me that life is without meaning and without joy. And to that I say, "Would you do one thing each day that makes you feel better? Will you accomplish one thing as small as it might be and center your attention on that accomplishment? Live each day as it comes."

You know we have a great ability to either put off and not live today or to worry and not live today. But, God would have us live each day taking it as a gift of His and moving on.

Then, lastly and by far the most important thing of all. If we're going to put worry behind us, we have to keep in touch with

God daily, for He is the source of our strength. Our worry and our anxieties, our tensions come to us by and large when we take our eyes and our attention away from the God, who loves us and cares for us, and we begin to center them on ourselves, our abilities and our limitations.

But, oh, if we keep in tune with God there can come and inner peace and an inner strength and a new direction in life - for He is our source of strength. He can heal the past sins and mistakes through forgiveness. He can guide us through tomorrow with his wisdom and He will always watch over us through each day.

So Jesus said, "Why be anxious about tomorrow?" Why let worry ruin your life? Keep in tune with your Heavenly Father. Let his spirit be your constant guide and strength. Let him be that in your life that makes you know that life is good and worth living. For God does love us. We can put worry behind us if we put God before us.

11.

NEW BEGINNINGS

Mark 10:46-52

Then they came to Jericho. As Jesus and his disciples, together with a large crowd, were leaving the city, a blind man, Bartimaeus (which means "son of Timaeus"), was sitting by the roadside begging. When he heard that it was Jesus of Nazareth, he began to shout, "Jesus, Son of David, have mercy on me!" Many rebuked him and told him to be quiet, but he shouted all the more, "Son of David, have mercy on me!" Jesus stopped and said, "Call him." So they called to the blind man, "Cheer up! On your feet! He's calling you." Throwing his cloak aside, he jumped to his feet and came to Jesus. "What do you want me to do for you?" Jesus asked him. The blind man said, "Rabbi, I want to see." "Go," said Jesus, "your faith has healed you." Immediately he received his sight and followed Jesus along the road.

One of the greatest things that can happen to us is for us to have "new beginnings." The scripture reminds us that we all have sinned. We have all failed God. We all need forgiveness and new beginnings. Not one new beginning but many new beginnings.

The New Testament is filled with the story of many new beginnings and the need for new beginnings. We could look at the Disciples and begin to see some of the new beginnings that took place in their lives. When they begin to follow Jesus Christ that was one new beginning. When they begin to see Jesus perform miracles, they began again another quest of understanding the power of God.

When they saw Jesus forgiving sinners, they began to grasp the meaning of forgiveness and the understanding of love. When Jesus told them of the cross, they did not understand but after the cross they begin again to understand the power of commitment. What it meant to be faithful and loyal yea even to death.

Or with the gift of the Holy Spirit, it was a new beginning of their concept of mission. Seeing the world as their parish, their place of ministry. We, like they, need many new beginnings. Not just one. But, we do not need to begin each time at the same place. We need to begin each time and move forward to a higher level of Christian commitment. We need to begin and move forward to a more Christlike life.

And so, there comes a question – what are the steps of the new beginnings that we can have that will make it effective in our lives? There are four steps I would lift up for us this morning.

First, we must begin by being aware of our needs. We can never move forward as Christians until we make the first step of being aware of the fact that we have need in our lives that we ourselves cannot meet.

I read to you this morning in the Scriptures of a story that is told in all the gospels in various forms. I read it from the Gospel of Mark because it means so much to me in this Gospel. This is the story of blind Bartimaeus. Bartimaeus, when he heard the trampling of the crowd as they were leaving Jericho and going to

Jerusalem, knew that something exciting was happening and so he began to ask, "What is going on?"

Someone said, "Jesus of Nazareth is passing by."

When he heard the word Jesus, he became aware of his needs. He was a blind beggar, sitting by the roadside. No one had ever been able to help him. And yet, he was aware that he had the need of sight. And so as Jesus approached he began to cry out, "Jesus, Son of David, have mercy on me."

In three of the Gospels they admonish him to be quiet. They tell him not to disturb the crowd. Jesus is on an important mission. He is going to Jerusalem (they thought to be crowned King). They weren't going to have a blind bagger to stop the process. But Bartimaeus cried out even louder until Jesus heard him above the noise of the crowd.

We must be aware of our needs. We must face the fact that we need someone to help us. Bartimaeus faced the fact that Jesus could help him.

Or, we find the story of Nicodemus. Nicodemus, a teacher, a leader in his own faith, was aware that there were parts of his understanding that were severely limited. And rather than risk criticism and ostracism of his fellow leaders he came to Jesus in the cover of night. But he was honest about the fact that he had needs. He was aware of his needs and he began the process of trying to find a way to meet them.

Or the story of the Rich Young Ruler. We see him come running to Jesus. He didn't just happen to be running down that road when Jesus passed. He sought Jesus out because he was aware of the need to feel the emptiness in his life. For him to begin again he knew that he had to begin with someone who knew more than he did.

Or the Prodigal Son and so we could go calling the roll of the people in the New Testament who faced themselves and realized that they needed something. You know there is something strange and something significant about all of us. All of us stand in need. I don't care who we are or how long we have lived or how deep our faith is or how shallow, we all stand in need of something.

And the one thing that the New Testament shares with us, with a great deal of clarity, is that there were those who became aware of their needs and they all turned to Jesus. Because they were aware that, somehow, the power of meeting those needs was not in their own lives. Maybe, just maybe, they could find the power in this man called Jesus.

The second step of new beginnings is not only to be aware of our needs but to voice them. To say something about them. To let the world know. Now sometimes when I say this people get the wrong idea. They think that the task is to tell folks their troubles. No, that is not it. There is plenty of that going on. People tell you their troubles and they don't want any change to happen in their life. The next day you meet them, and they've still got the same trouble. And the next year you meet them, and they've still got the same trouble. They drag it around like a badge. "I've got a problem," they say.

That is not what I'm talking about. I am saying that we need to voice our needs with an awareness that something can be done. Blind Bartimaeus didn't disturb the crowd saying, "I'm blind." He disturbed the crowd because he cried out for help from Jesus. They would have given him trinkets to keep him quiet, but he didn't want the same thing, the same problem year in and year out. He wanted to begin to find a solution to that problem. He wanted to begin to see. To begin life anew. And so as he wanted to begin life anew he cried out for help to someone that could help him. Believing that He could help him. And he wouldn't quit until he found help.

Nicodemus we see the same way. He didn't look at his mind and his heart and say, "I'm puzzled by some things that are happening in God's world and I don't understand them," and stop there. But he came to Jesus and said, "Explain to me how the new birth takes place. Tell me what the power of God can do for my life?" He voiced his need.

We in America have a tremendous ability to suppress the needs that we have and not tell anyone our true hurts. We've learned not to share the depth of our soul; but we are the loser when we have done this. Oh, how we need to come before our Lord and pour out to Him the heartaches and the problems that we face.

How we need to come and voice to him the care and concern that we have, for we'll never move past the problem that we have until we come and honestly voice it in prayer and through sharing it.

You know sometimes we are like an ostrich. We like to play that if we stick our head in the sand that when we take our head up the problem is gone. It does it doesn't disappear that way. If we want to have a new beginning that makes life fresh and meaningful we not only have to see our needs but we have to share it with God.

Share it with a Christian friend who, in honesty, will love and pray and care for you or you can honestly love and pray and share with them. But there is a need in our day of voicing the hurts in our lives, the needs that we have.

The third step is equally as important, maybe even more so. After we've faced our needs and after we've voiced our needs, then we need to act on the situation. When Bartimaeus sat on the side of the road crying out, "Jesus, Son of David, have mercy on me," he was voicing his need. But when the word was passed back to him, "Hurry up, come to Jesus." There is an interesting line in the Gospel of Mark. It said, "He threw off his mantle." He threw off the one thing that would keep him from getting to Jesus. Remember Bartimaeus was blind and the mantle was a long coat that reached down to his ankles. And if a blind man was trying to run to meet someone that was waiting for him he wanted to throw aside all the obstacles that would keep him from Jesus.

For us to have new beginnings in the Christian faith there comes a time when we have to throw off the obstacles that keep us from moving forward as Christians. It is not always easy to throw off those obstacles because they become so important to us. You know, Bartimaeus did not have but one mantle probably. One coat. He didn't have but one long coat to keep him warm on the cold days that he had to sit out there in the drizzling rain and beg for his bread. It was all he had. It would've been so easy for him to have said, "I can't give up my coat. I don't care if Jesus is waiting for me. I'll just take my own time and my own way."

Friend, he didn't believe that his coat was going to give him sight; he believed Jesus was. When we come to believe that Jesus can, through his love and power of love and forgiveness and healing begin to make life new for us –a new beginning - we don't have to hold onto the old scraps of life that were meaningful to us before the light of his love touched our hearts. We don't have to hold onto our old thoughts and our old plans and our old dreams that block us from Jesus. We must act on the situation.

And Bartimaeus threw off the cloak and Nicodemus came to Jesus. He acted on the situation, knowing full well that he would be criticized in the Sanhedrin. The Prodigal Son acted on the situation when he faced his need. When he voiced it to himself, knowing full well that when he got back home he might not be accepted back as a son. But he acted because he believed that there was something there for him better than the pigpen of life. There was a point of new beginning and he acted.

Then the last point of our new beginnings in life has to come as the willingness to follow. Probably the saddest of all the stories of the New Testament is the story of the Rich Young Ruler who came to Jesus. Now he faced his need. He voiced his need. He acted on his need. He ran to Jesus but when he got there and Jesus challenged him he went away sorrowfully because he refused the challenge.

You know for new beginnings, there have to be some things that we have to take a step of faith on. We have to launch on something that we have never done before. Otherwise, it is not a new beginning. It's an old beginning that we have tried time and time again.

The Rich Young Ruler wanted an easy answer. He wanted Jesus to say to him, "Son, it's all right. You can be just like you have been doing." But the tragedy of the story would have been that the emptiness in him would have remained. And so will it with us.

I see people day in and day out who come to the verge of following Jesus in a new dimension of life but then all of a sudden they realize that it costs them something. It costs them something of a new pattern, a new direction, a new hope, a new lifestyle. And all of a sudden they say, "It's too expensive."

But I love the story of Bartimaeus because the closing line of the story tells the real heart of the man. He cried out for help until he got it. He moved aside every obstacle that would keep him from getting to Jesus and getting the new help but as soon as he got it he didn't go back to his old way of life. The lovely line is, "He followed in the Way." We don't know what happened to Bartimaeus but you know I wonder how many people's lives were touched and changed and transformed because this man and his new beginning didn't just express the need and cry out for help and go to Jesus but as soon as Jesus touched his life he followed him, day by day.

New beginnings we all need. We all need to see the new dimensions of life that Christ would transform and redeem in us. We all need to face honestly the deep needs of our hearts and minds and souls. But most important, when we have done all the homework. When we have knelt in prayer. When we have shared with God all our thoughts and our dreams and our plans and our hurts, then there comes the time for action. The time of following. Learning, as Jesus did, to say, "Not my will but Thy will." Learning like blind Bartimaeus, who could now see that there is a new road to follow.

The Christian faith doesn't begin with just one new beginning and end there. It begins with a new beginning but down the road of life there dozens of new beginnings for everyone of us. Where the spirit of God sweeps over our lives with a new and dynamic way and points to a fullness of life.

If we are willing to follow, we like Bartimaeus can learn to see a new dimension of life. New beginnings – there is something about every human being that loves new beginnings. The new year, the new day, the new season and so it is with the soul there comes so many times when God challenges us to follow him in a new direction. With a new commitment. With a new loyalty that our lives might be filled with the richness of His love.

As we face our needs, as we voice them, as we share them, I pray that we will have the strength to follow as Christ would lead us in a more committed path of life that leads to Him.

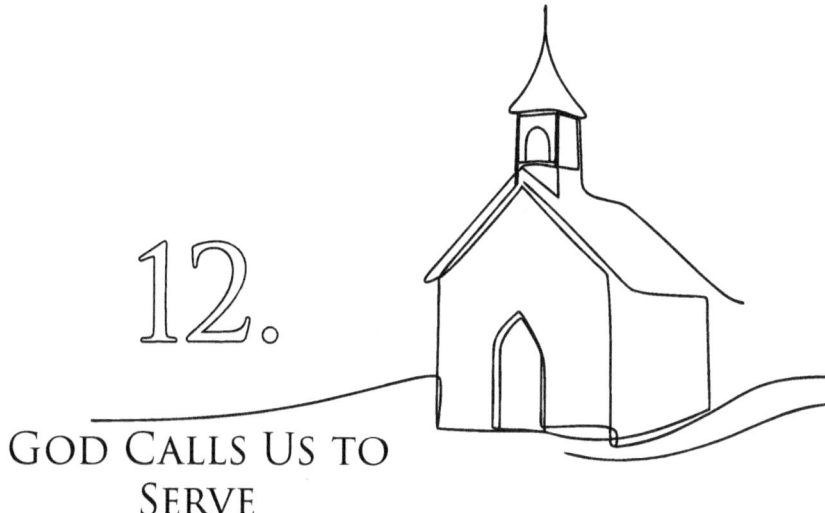

12.

GOD CALLS US TO SERVE

NOTE 1: As a point of historical context this sermon was likely delivered in early 1983.

NOTE 2: This is the only sermon I discovered with no biblical text indicated. At the end, I selected two short verses from Matthew that seemed to fit the message.

Today I want to deal with two things: the charges that have been brought against the ecumenical ministries of the church – the National Council, and the World Council of Churches – and how these charges relate to our church, and then I want to deal with our sermon title this morning, "God Calls Us to Serve."

The charges that have been brought against the National and World Councils of Churches have been brought by *Reader's Digest* in two articles – the latest was in January – and by *60 Minutes,* which is a television program sponsored by CBS. The title of the *Reader's Digest* article was a question, "Do You Know Where Your Church Offerings Go?" And then there is a very suggestive warning in the sub-title, "You Had Better Find Out . . . Because They May Be Supporting Revolution Instead of Religion." Now there were several questions raised in this article, and I would like to deal with them in four broad areas this morning. I cannot in an hour's time give you an exhaustive set of answers for all the questions raised, but I can give you some answers in some broad areas that will allow you to get a picture of their mind-set and their thinking. I'd like to deal with the area of Vietnam, our relationship with Christians in Cuba, some questions they lifted about Nicaragua, and the question of the church's activities in Africa.

First of all, *60 Minutes* and *Reader's Digest* made some conflicting statements about what had happened in Vietnam, but these discrepancies are not our concern here. The implication was that we Methodists had, through, the National Council of Churches, and the World Council of Churches, and the Church World Service, given monies to the Communist government of Vietnam. I'll give you the facts: Church World Service sent $500,000 to Viet Nam to buy food and medicine for people in hospitals, children in orphanages, and people in refugee camps. Harry Haines, the president of the United Methodist Committee on Relief sent five churchmen to supervise the distribution of this food. It went where it was supposed to go. The people making the charge have not been there to see how the money was spent – they simply said we sent money to the Communist government.

Another charge having to do with Vietnam was that the church had sent $179,000 to camps that the Communists were using to retrain some of the Vietnamese people. We did send that much money - not our church - but the ecumenical church. It was sent at the request of the 2,000,000+ Christians in Vietnam who asked us to send them seeds and tools so that we could give them a hand - not a handout. I don't believe there's a person in this sanctuary who would have us do anything less than what we did there. We fed the hungry. We gave medicine to the sick. We gave hope to the people whose land had been ravished by war for all these years and we gave them seeds and tools to start again. I am appalled that anyone would throw stones at the ecumenical church for being compassionate. And I cannot understand it anyway how someone could criticize one Christian congregation for reaching out to another Christian congregation, saying, "Here will give you a helping hand." That is what happened in Vietnam. These are verifiable facts by the National Council Churches, Church World Service and the United Methodist Committee on Relief. A recent edition of *U.S. News & World Report* has had a good article on what has actually happened in Vietnam.

The second charge by *60 Minutes* and *Reader's Digest* had to do with Cuba. There were two areas that they concentrated on in what we were doing in Cuba. The first was the Cuban reunification plan. The Methodist Church - not the ecumenical church - <u>our</u> church spent $15,000 in this program whose purpose was to reunite families that had been split up because they were fleeing from Communism. Family members were in Miami and Dade County, and the surrounding area, and they didn't know each other's whereabouts. Through Bishop Hunt's office in Orlando, Florida, this money was used to help these people find their families. I don't see anything dark and sinister about that. They were not Communists infiltrating our land, these were Christians had lost their families. Thank God our church had enough compassion to reach out and reunite them.

Another allegation dealing with Cuba was that the Cuban Resource Center in New York was some subversive operation through which we funneled money to the Cuban government. Well, now ladies, I'll have to say that you are the only ones who gave anything to that operation because you are part of the United Methodist Women and they gave $38,500 in 1971. Thank God for you! The purpose of this center is to get information about human rights and what was happening in Cuba to other Cubans who had fled Communism. It was renewed in 1979, and they have been basically self-supporting since then, but the Methodist women have given them $750 in the last three years, and I thank you for it. Now those are the facts.

The third area where our giving was questioned is Nicaragua. There have been two charges about Nicaragua, too. One was that through the literacy program, we were paying Communists or Communist sympathizers to teach in Nicaragua. The National Council of Churches has been involved in a program of lifting the level of literacy in Nicaragua since the fall of the Somoza government. At that junction only 30% of the people in Nicaragua could read and write. Today, a near miracle, 80% can read and write. We've had some small part in that. Morley Safer of *60 Minutes* endeavored to imply that Americans were not wanted and would be in danger there. There are approximately 1,000 Americans there teaching literacy now in private organizations - not the church. They remain there and apparently do not feel endangered.

Another item about Nicaragua that was lifted up was dealing with the Institute of Economics and Social Research in Nicaragua. The Board of Global Ministries gave $60,000 for this institute so that they could gather leaders throughout Latin America to discuss and develop plans for a viable democracy for the Latin American countries. This program was under the supervision of the University of Texas and partially funded by the United States government. I don't understand why this program was attacked - but it was.

Lastly, there is the charge that in the unrest and foment in Africa, Methodist were aiding and abetting the revolutionaries. Statements even have been made that we had bought guns! Not one document has been produced by CBS, *Readers Digest*, or anyone else that one dollar of church contributions has been spent for guns. The answer comes from Reverend Ted Wolfe, a missionary in Africa, who said, "The Chinese and Russians are happy to buy guns. The money you send will be used in a refugee camp."

Why the charges? Charges inflame people's emotions. They sell magazines and up the rating of television programs. These charges were made against the National Council of Churches, the World Council of Churches and the United Methodist Church. We were, by the way, the only denomination mentioned by name in any of the charges, though many denominations contributed to the Councils.

As an Example of CBS's ethics *60 Minutes* is in contempt of a New Orleans court for broadcasting their "exposé" in that area. A trial was in progress at the city dealing with issues that were aired on the program, and the judge felt the jury might be influenced by the broadcast, and so ruled the tape of the program should not be released until the trial has been completed. He brought the lawyers representing CBS in and told them that he, in all his life, had never encountered such outrageous conduct toward the judicial system. In the February 10th *Mobile Press Register* newspaper, he is quoted as saying that the maximum sentence shall be given to CBS for their blatant attitude of disrespect for the law.

The bottom line therefore is dollar and cents. The church is not going to sue CBS. The church is not going to sue *Readers Digest*. We are supposed to be a loving and gentle and forgiving people. And so once again the powers of big business have exploited the American public and wounded the body of Christ for the gain of the almighty dollar.

I would remind you that the *Readers Digest* has put out a condensed version of the Bible. Who gives it the right to mutilate the scriptures? No council has ever dared have the audacity to take scissors and cut from the scriptures the things that they didn't think were worth printing. But *Readers Digest* has, so that they might sell a product and make more money. Tragic.

Those are the charges. You know what our church has done. You see where our church has been ministering. But no worship service should be left at this point. There comes a challenge to us.

We are called to serve. I want to say to you this morning that I have <u>never</u> been prouder to be a United Methodist than I am today. I stand with pride, and I say I'm part of a church that ministers to the hungry, the needy, the hopeless and the dejected. Thank God the church is there with them. My church and your church. We are called to serve. We are called to minister.

Wednesday, as I drove back from the Bishop's Convocation, I begin to think about ministering to the people who stand in desperate need. And I began to ask myself, "How long has it been, Tom, since you have walked into a home when there is absolutely no food, carrying a bag of groceries under your arm, sit it down on the table and hold a little child that's crying until its mother is able to fix it something to eat because it has not had food in 24 hours?" And then I begin to realize how comfortable I had gotten. How comfortable you loving people have made me down through the years. How comfortable all of us have gotten. How we have forgotten the hurts and the loneliness and the brokenness of life that is out there.

Then I am reminded of the story of the minister who was sent to a downtown church in Chicago in the middle of the ghetto. The first Sunday when it was time for him to go and pray with the choir, and then into the service, they couldn't find him. They sent an usher out to look through all the rooms; at last they found him. He was in his study standing looking out the window at the slum area of Chicago, and he was crying. The usher said to him, "Sir, the service . . ." and he didn't answer. He said to him again, "Sir, the service," and then the usher realized what was happening and he said, "Sir, you'll get used to it." The minister turned to him and said, "That's why I'm crying - I know I'll get used to it."

If these articles and this TV show have done anything for me they have made me aware that I've gotten used to the suffering and the hurt of humanity, and that I've forgotten that God has called me to minister to the brokenness of life. Brokenness that is so great that sometimes our minds cannot quite conceive above it. But it's there.

Then I begin to think about what was going to happen to those people scattered around the world in their abject poverty in need. Because these articles that were written and this TV show that was shown is going to hurt the body of Christ at the place where it can least afford to be hurt. These people who have, at best, a crust of bread. These orphans have little or nothing. Their resources, except by the grace of God, shall be dried up because of these demonic statements of the apostles of discord.

I thought about this all day Friday as I drove to Atlanta to visit my wife, Ann, who was hospitalized there. Friday night I said to her, "What are we going to do? I want to take an offering Sunday for World Hunger. I don't know how much we can give - I don't know what our bills are going to be." She looked at me and she said, "You know what the nature of the church is. You know what our mission is, I want you to give whatever we can." Well, I wrestled with this idea, and I thought of a few dollars here and a few dollars there, and then yesterday morning she said. "I believe in seed faith money. Give until it hurts because we've never been hungry - but these people are." And then I felt like Jeremiah: "Lord, what can we do?"

We little handful of folks in Brewton, Alabama who call ourselves the body of Christ. The word has gone out across the whole of the land in one direction. What can we do? Then there came to me an awareness that God has not limited us to these four walls to minister. I promise you that when the final "Amen" is said and when we walk out the door, whatever we give to World Hunger today - I'm going to write a letter to the Bishop and challenge him to challenge every United Methodist Church in our area to reach out in love and compassion to God's people who stand in the greatest need. That's what it's all about. God has reached down in love to minister to us and sometimes we forget the hurt and the needy around the world.

Eldridge Cleaver, this man who disdained our system and went out across the world to find the "great society" came back to say that the poverty-stricken of America were crushed between silk sheets. What he was saying was that you cannot imagine the poverty in Latin America and South America and East Asia and Africa. Our minds have no way of grasping the living conditions of these people that God is calling us to serve.

As I drove home yesterday afternoon, I begin to think about what had been my ministry through all these years. My mind went back to a rainy November night to the basement of the church where the MYF group (Methodist Youth Foundation) was meeting in a little Methodist Church. And I heard someone read the passage of scripture from Luke where Jesus said he was called to bind up the broken of life, to set at liberty those who were held captive. And from that moment until now, I have not been my own, but I've been his. Now, sometimes I have to confess that I have been too much my own and not enough his, but I believe that we as God's people need to answer the challenge of ministry and the pride of being a part of a church who cares by saying we are in the business of binding up the brokenness of life.

So, in a minute we are going to take the offering, and when we take the offering if you want to give something to World Hunger there's an envelope in the pew in front of you. Take it and write on it World Hunger and put in whatever you want to. Know that you're going to be feeding someone who would be hungry if you didn't feed them. I don't take special offerings very often, for two or three reasons. I take very seriously the commitment that is given when you say what you plan to give to the life of the church for the year. And the other is that sometimes it's dangerous to take special offerings.

One time, one year in my life, I served a church that didn't pay all of its World Service. It couldn't. In fact, it couldn't pay me part of the time. But I couldn't go to Annual Conference and say that my church hadn't done anything for World Service. And so, on the Sunday night before I went to Annual Conference, I said, "We're going to take a special offering for World Service later tonight. I don't know how many are going to be here - you know how many come on Sunday night - and I don't know how much you're going to give, but I'm going give you an opportunity."

That night the regular handful, and maybe a few extra, gathered in this little church. And when the ushers were taking the offering, I bowed my head because I was afraid to look to see if anyone was putting anything in the plate at all. And then I began to hear the sound of coins - a whole bunch of coins - being poured into the plate. My curiosity got the best of me. I lifted my eyes and looked out, and I've never stood taller. I saw my five-year-old son emptying everything he had and his piggy bank into that offering plate. And after we got home I said, "Son, why did you do that?" And he said, "Daddy, it was important."

What we are doing today is important. It's important to know that we are about the task of ministering to God's broken people. And we are not ashamed when there are those who throw stones at the ministry of the church to the poverty-stricken the world. We can stand with pride and say, "Through God's grace, we can minister." There is healing power in the Lord Jesus Christ that can heal the brokenness of life and thank God he is given us part in the healing process.

"I was hungry and you gave me food, I was thirsty, and you gave me drink, I was a stranger, and you welcomed me, I was naked, and you clothed me, I was sick, and you visited me, I was in prison, and you came to me." Jesus

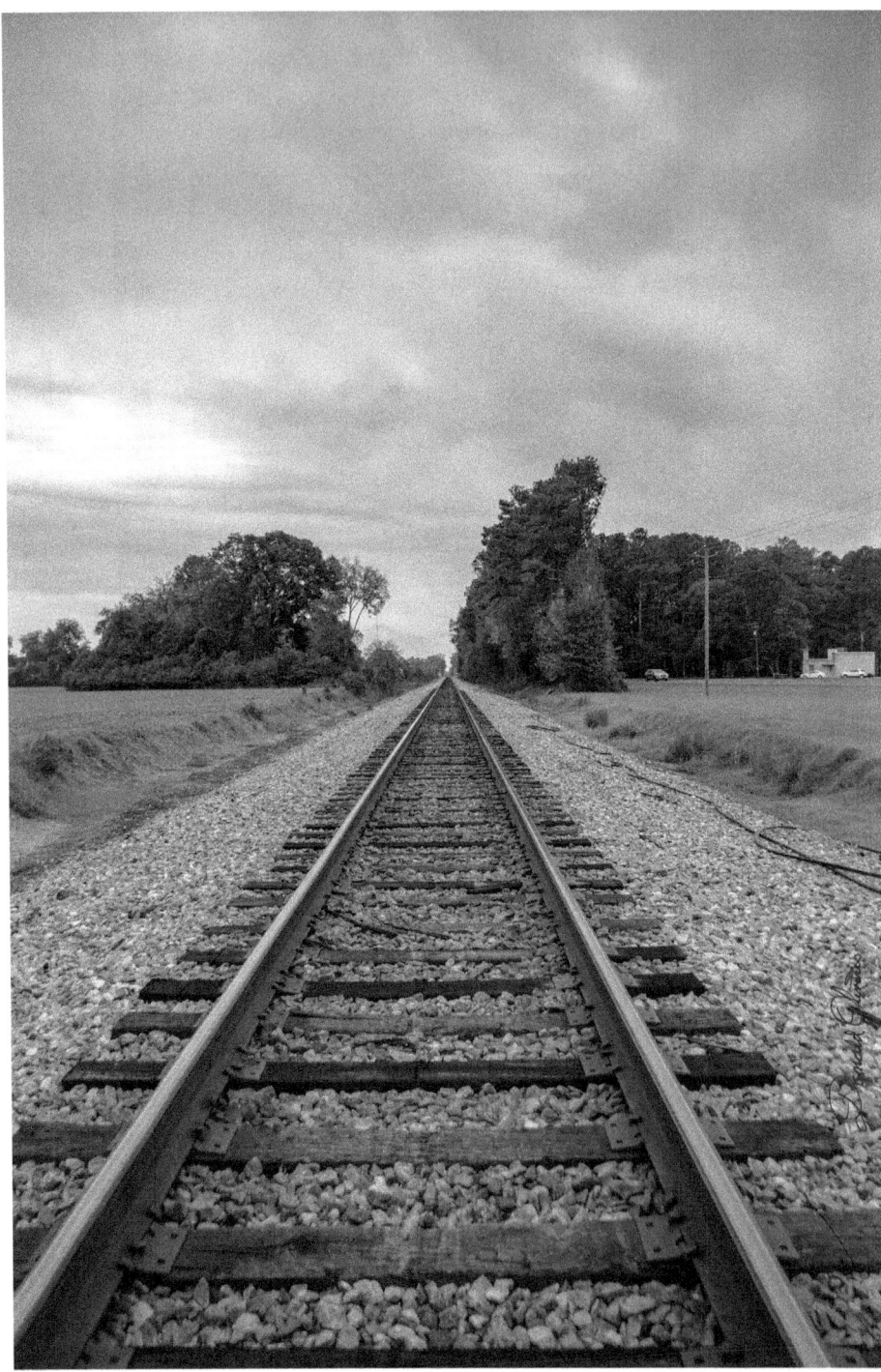

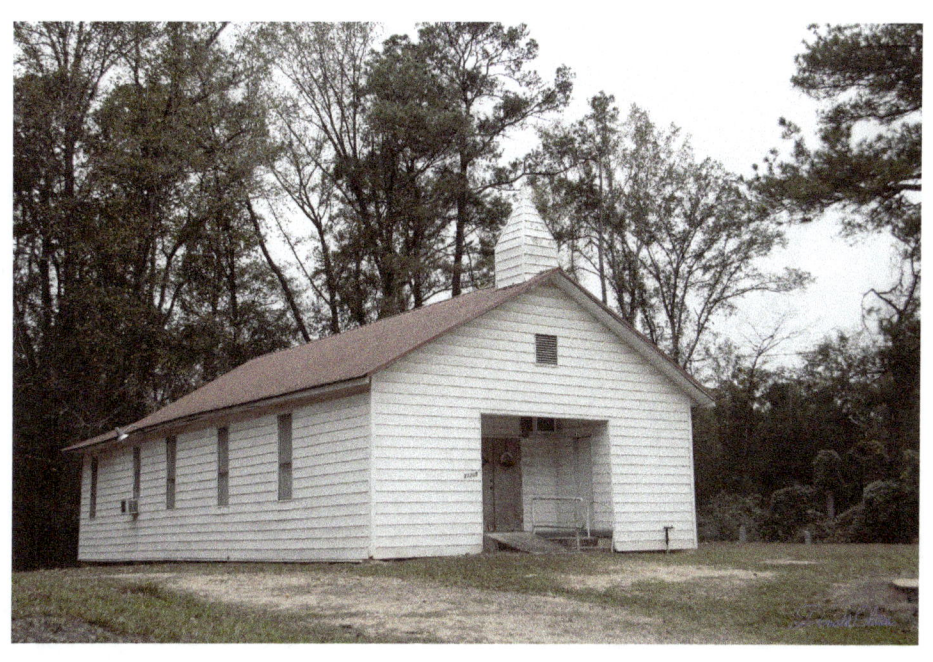

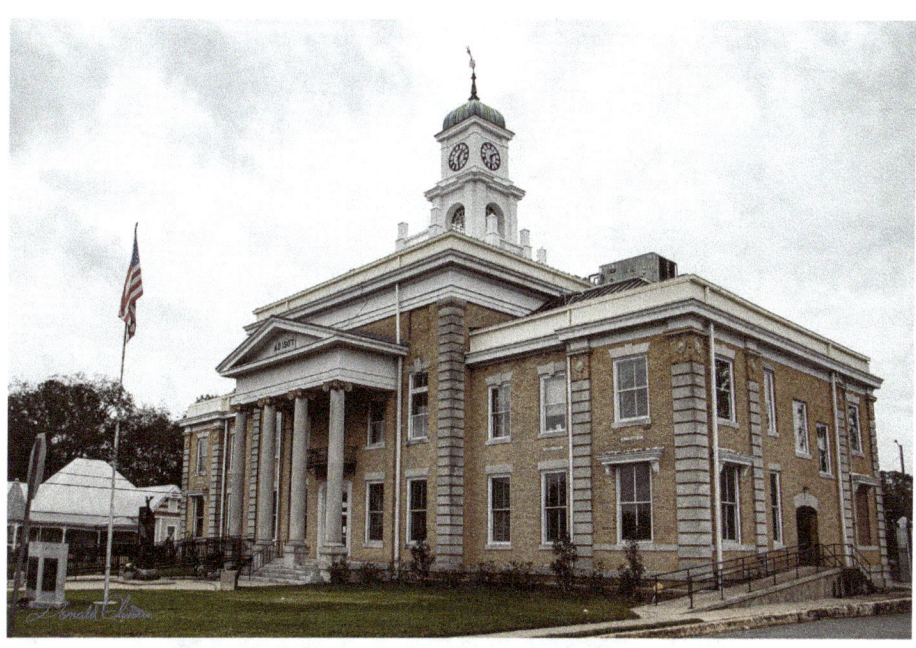

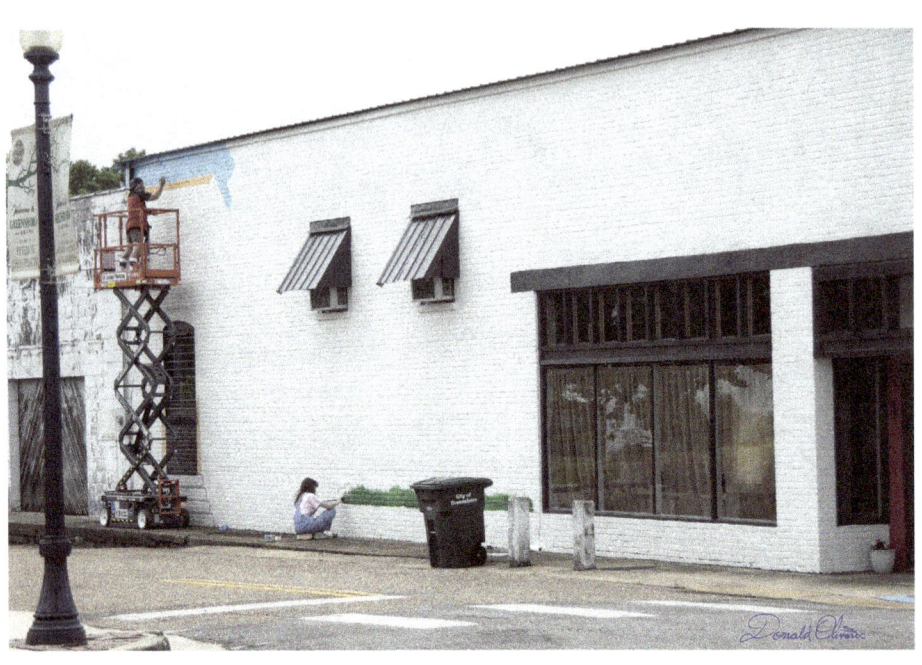

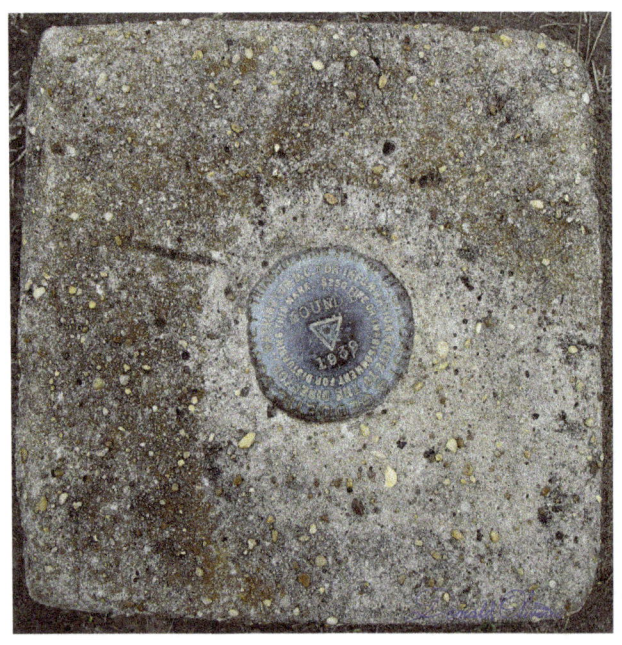

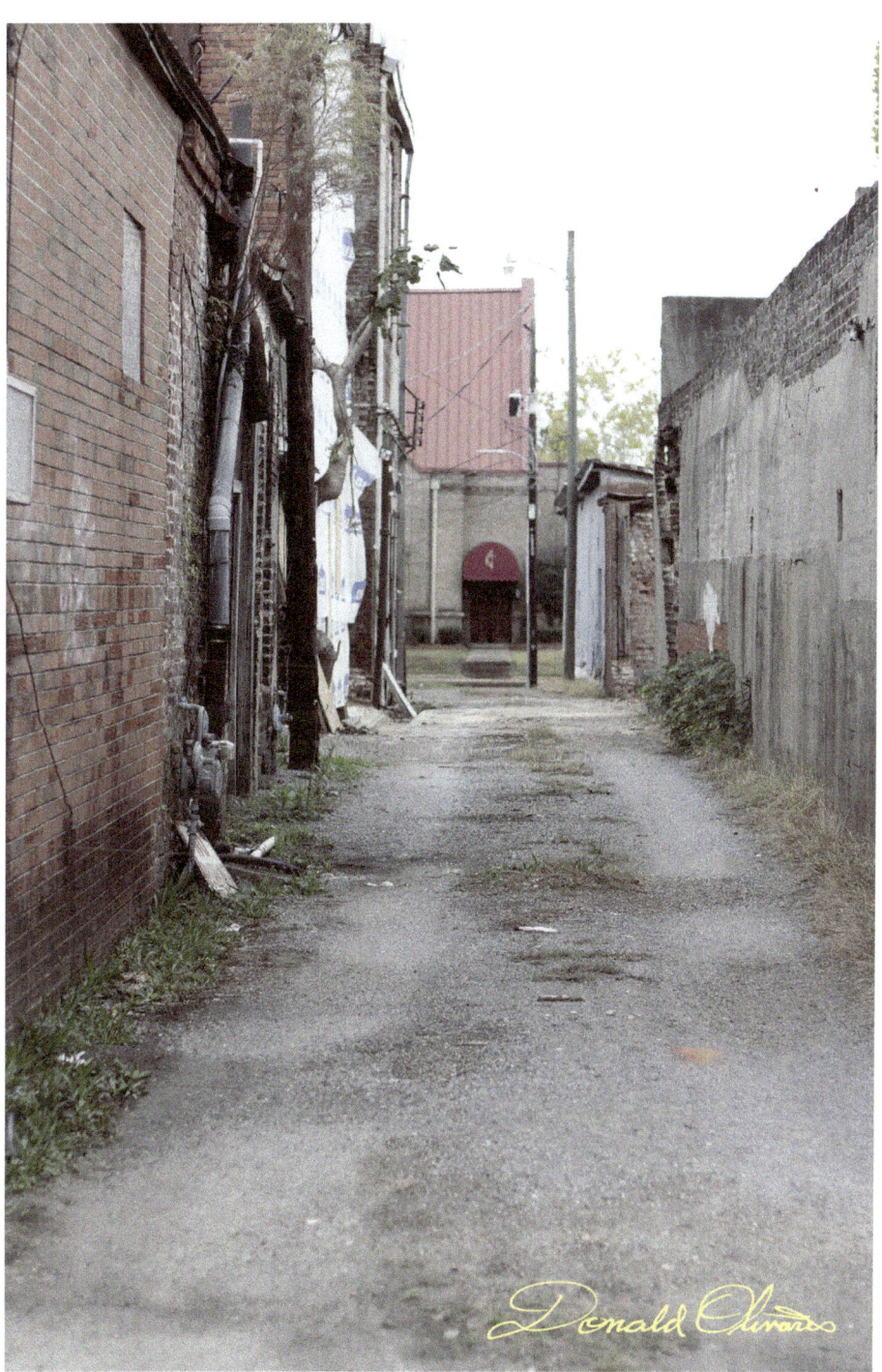

Appendix: Methodist Churches served by J. Thomas Terry (1956–2007)#

When	Where	Church
1956	Maplesville, AL	Maplesville Ct.
	Randolph, AL	Cox Chapel
1958	Divinity Student at Emory (Atlanta, GA)	NONE
1959	Divinity Student at Vanderbilt University (Nashville, TN)	
	Gallatin, TN	Gallatin UMC
	Carro, TN ?	Carro UMC ?
	Castalian Springs, TN	Castalian Springs UMC
1960	Catherine, AL	Gastonburg UMC
	Central Mills/Safford, AL	Center Chapel UMC
	Magnolia, AL	Magnolia UMC
	Rebotec, AL ?	Rebotec UMC ?
1962	Mt. Vernon, AL	Aldersgate UMC
1966	Tillmans Corner, AL	Grace UMC
1967	Grove Hill, AL	Grove Hill UMC
	Near Fulton, AL	Evans Chapel UMC
1972	Mobile, AL	South Brookley UMC
	Fowl River, AL	Fowl River UMC (now New Hope UMC)

1979	Prattville, AL	Trinity UMC
1982	Brewton, AL	1st Methodist Church of Brewton
1985	Mobile, AL	Forest Hill UMC
1990	Selma, AL	Church Street UMC
1991	Moundville, AL	Moundville UMC
	Moundville, AL	Stewart UMC
	Moundville, AL	China Grove UMC
	Moundville, AL	Havana UMC
	Moundville, AL	Pleasant Hill UMC ?
2001	Sweet Water, AL	Sweet Water UMC
2003	Greensboro, AL	Mount Hermon UMC
	Greensboro, AL	Ramey's Chapel UMC
2007	Retired (for the third and final time after retiring in 2001 and again in 2003)	

It is very likely that several smaller churches he served are not on this list

www.ingramcontent.com/pod-product-compliance
Lightning Source LLC
Chambersburg PA
CBHW051540170526
45165CB00002B/818